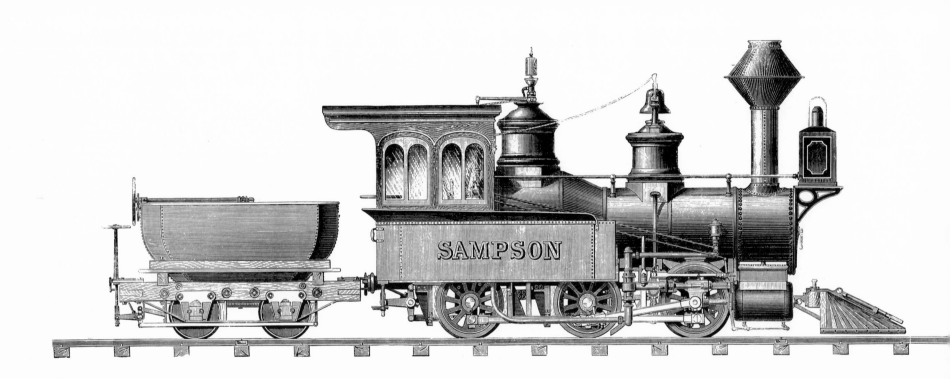

Early American
LOCOMOTIVES

with 147 Engravings

by

JOHN H. WHITE, JR.

Chairman, Dept. of Industries, Smithsonian Institution

DOVER PUBLICATIONS, INC., NEW YORK

FOR THOMAS NORRELL

Published in Canada by General Publishing
Company, Ltd., 30 Lesmill Road, Don Mills,
Toronto, Ontario.
Published in the United Kingdom by Constable
and Company, Ltd., 10 Orange Street, London WC 2.

Early American Locomotives: with 147 Engravings
is a new work, first published by Dover Publications, Inc., in 1972.

International Standard Book Number: 0-486-22772-3
Library of Congress Catalog Card Number: 79-18895

Manufactured in the United States of America
Dover Publications, Inc.
180 Varick Street
New York, N. Y. 10014

INTRODUCTION

This volume presents a collection of reproductions of the more decorative locomotive engravings published during the late nineteenth century, with emphasis on American locomotives. We will not offer a formal history in these pages, but a list of references is included for those seeking more information on the development of the railway engine.

The illustrations are drawn almost entirely from the engineering trade press, most particularly from the *Railroad Gazette* and *Engineering*, both of which produced folio-size collections of the better plates appearing in their respective pages. The *Railroad Gazette's* collection, first published in 1883 under the title *Recent Locomotives*, treated both domestic and foreign engines; it is from the greatly enlarged second edition of 1886 that we have reproduced so many of the plates in the present volume. Matthias N. Forney (1835–1908), editor of the *Gazette* when this book was produced, was a respected expert on railroad machinery, who had worked as a locomotive designer as a young man. During these years he obtained patents for a peculiar style of tank locomotive that came to bear his name, and therefore the extended space devoted to this design in *Recent Locomotives* is not difficult to understand. After 1870, the year in which Forney became associate editor of the *Gazette*, his rise in railway engineering circles was rapid; he was soon an officer in several national engineering societies. His *Catechism of the Locomotive Engine* (1874) went through many editions and became the basic American handbook on that subject. The present volume contains several reproductions from the *Catechism* and from a historical catalog Forney prepared in 1886 for the Rogers Locomotive Works; both of these works are now rare.

The other primary source for the present illustrations was produced by the British journal, *Engineering*. Entitled *A Record of The Transportation Exhibits at the World's Columbian Exposition of 1893*, this 779-page tome presented in pictures and text a very full account of the transportation machinery exhibits gathered at Chicago to celebrate the four-hundredth anniversary of Columbus' first landing. As it happened, the fair opened a year late, but no matter—it was a stupendous attraction that drew thousands of visitors and exhibitors to Chicago's lake front. Among the exhibitors were locomotive manufacturers, the Baltimore and Ohio Railroad and a few foreign railways. The manufacturers, obviously interested in showing their latest wares, featured engines known as compound locomotives because they used the steam twice before exhausting it to the atmosphere. Great fuel economies were claimed for these locomotives, but the additional machinery necessary cancelled the savings. However, the design, essentially a European development, was just gaining favor in the United States when the fair opened, and each builder was anxious to show off his particular type of compounding.

The Baldwin Locomotive Works, as might be expected from the leading American manufacturer, had the largest exhibit, consisting of sixteen engines. The Brooks Works of Dunkirk, New York, showed eight, while most of the other major builders were content to send only one or two machines. Several tiny industrial locomotives of the H. K. Porter Company were entered, though they must have seemed dwarfed alongside the giant main-line engines. The B & O Railroad took for itself the job of portraying the locomotive's historical development through a series of original and full-size wooden models, which were so skillfully done that they fooled "even the very elect." Some of the engravings dutifully made of the replicas for *Engineering*'s book are included in our first part, Historical Locomotives. In all, 62 locomotives were shown at the Columbian Exposition.

James Dredge (1840–1906), the author of this heroic volume on the exhibition, was something of a hero himself, at least to the world of engineering. Coming from a family of engineers, he first worked under the great British locomotive expert Daniel K. Clark. In 1866 he joined Zehra Colburn, the American journalist who founded *Engineering* magazine in London, and after Colburn's suicide in 1870, Dredge became a joint owner of the magazine. Dredge showed a particular interest in the world's fairs so prevalent during the last century, filling the pages of *Engineering* with descriptions of the wonders to be seen in Vienna 1873, Philadelphia 1876, Paris 1879 and elsewhere. In 1893 he was appointed British Commissioner to the World's Columbian Exposition, and this event he chronicled most completely, as already noted. Many honors came to Dredge late in his life, including two Legion of Honor awards.

We have reproduced engravings from several other technical publications in addition to the sources already noted. The temptation was present to introduce materials from the popular papers of the period, such as *Harpers,* or the colorful prints of Currier and Ives, but these views are generally incorrect or imaginary, charming as they may be. For the sake of accuracy, therefore, we preferred to confine our presentation to those materials available in the engineering press.

Engravings were the only practical form of printed illustration before the introduction of the cheap halftone process in the 1890's. Hundreds of artisans were employed throughout the land preparing line cuts for newspaper, magazine, book and catalog illustrations. These illustrations might be cut or engraved on wood, copper, or steel—the finer, more detailed drawings usually being done on metal plates. Some were drawn from nature or the artist's imagination, but much of the work was copied directly from photographs. This was more convenient than traveling to the prototype and more accurate than working from a sketch. The artist may have been only a copyist, but the precision of his images reflects a fine drafting skill, particularly in illustrations of machinery. An example of an engraving that agrees exactly with the surviving photograph is given.

Because we expect this book to be of interest to the artist, a few remarks on the finish and painting of locomotives are included here. The cheap locomotive prints which are available today as decorator items are sometimes mechanically accurate, many being reproduced from the originals, but the colors are often grotesque misrepresentations of the actual finishes. Sometimes the coloring is undoubtedly inspired by the garishly decorated locomotives seen on tourist railways or television dramas; sometimes it can be blamed on the printers' indifference. But in nearly all cases there is too much color. Even at the high point of locomotive decoration in the 1850's, a relatively small part of the locomotive was painted; most of the machinery was polished metal, while the dome and cylinder covers, together with most small fittings, were bright brass. The boiler was covered in russia iron, a shiny rust-resistant sheet metal which came in many hues ranging from brown to blue, but was commonly a silver grey hue. Red paint was often used on the wheels, cowcatcher and cab, or just on the wheels with the cab and cowcatcher painted green. Sometimes the cab was in a natural wood finish of walnut, oak or cherry. The striping and ornamentation were delicate and finely shaded, and never done in a clumsy, circus-wagon style that is too often employed in modern imitations of the original livery.

It was only from about 1845 to 1870 that this highly elaborate style of painting was in fashion; bright colors appear to have been used previously, but the general decorative treatment was more restrained. Actually there is relatively little information available on the subject of color until the late 1840's when locomotive builders began to produce full-color lithographs of their products, which clearly document the desire for more ornamental machines. However, highly finished locomotives fell from favor during the 1860's, primarily because of cost; another factor was the introduction of coal burning and its sooty smoke which soon covered the

Photograph and engraving of Baldwin's *Consolidation*, showing the accuracy of the artist's illustration technique.

engine's brightwork with a stubborn grime. During the next two decades the brightly finished locomotive vanished from the American scene, replaced by the business-like engine with more and more of its exterior painted black. Gone were the elaborate architectural features, much of the brass, and all of the bright paint. By the 1890's some roads were eliminating the lustre of the russia iron in favor of painted black sheet metal coverings. Only the connecting rods and a few other incidental bright steel or brass accessories, such as the bell and whistle, offered any contrast to the sombre black machine.

This book has been arranged in four sections in an effort to divide the locomotives into logical groupings by date, type or place of service. The division is somewhat arbitrary, and some machines might logically fit in two or more categories, but the arrangement should at least help to emphasize the major classifications for those not well acquainted with the subject. In addition to the earliest locomotives, the historical chapter also includes some machines whose design was antique even for their date of construction; the Eddy Clock is a case in point. The second chapter encompasses typical main-line freight and passenger engines for the years 1870 to 1895. The oddities, industrial and switching engines, are dealt with in the third chapter, which also might have included some of the machines shown in Chapter 1, as mentioned in the captions. The last chapter indicates what was going on elsewhere in the world. The export engines, it might be noted, are almost entirely standard American designs with necessary modifications for overseas service.

Because our presentation is confined to engravings it logically ends in the 1890's when the widespread practice of that art died.

The system used to classify the locomotives in these pages is easily explained. The basic classification for locomotives is by wheel arrangement. Since the beginnings of steam railroads, an indication of the number of wheels has been the commonest method of communication between locomotive men; such a simple description as "ten wheeler" conveys a clear picture of the general arrangement and even the approximate size and type of service of the locomotive to anyone familiar with the subject. Errors are possible, however, for a ten wheeler could could mean an engine with four leading and six driving wheels (4–6–0) or an engine with ten driving wheels (0–10–0) or even a machine with two leading and eight driving wheels, (2–8–0) although the term is commonly understood to mean the first-mentioned type. To avoid such misunderstanding the wheel arrangement classes were formalized into a three-number system by a New York Central mechanical official, Frederic M. Whyte (1865–1941), in 1900.

The first figure in the three-number symbol indicates the number of leading wheels, the second figure the number of driving wheels and the final figure the number of trailing wheels. Using the ten wheeler as an example, if we had four leading wheels, six driving wheels and no trailing wheels, the Whyte symbol would be 4–6–0.

In addition to wheel counting, certain types of locomotives also acquired class names, which are used interchangeably with the Whyte symbols. The more common names are listed below, including those which were developed in the twentieth century and are not therefore represented in the present volume.

WHYTE CLASSIFICATION SYSTEM

Whyte Symbol	*Class Name*
2–6–0	Mogul
2–6–2	Prairie
2–4–2	Columbia
2–8–0	Consolidation
2–10–0	Decapod
2–10–2	Santa Fe
2–10–4	Texas
4–4–0	American
4–4–2	Atlantic
4–6–0	Ten Wheeler
4–6–2	Pacific
4–6–4	Hudson
4–8–0	Twelve Wheeler
4–8–2	Mountain
4–8–4	Northern
4–10–0	Mastodon
0–4–4	Forney

SUGGESTED READINGS

Ahrons, E. L. *The British Steam Railway Locomotive 1825–1925*. London: Locomotive Publishing Co., 1927.

Alexander, E. P. *Iron Horses*. New York: W. W. Norton & Co., 1941.

Brown, William H. *The History of the First Locomotive in America*. Revised ed. New York: D. Appleton & Co., 1874.

Bruce, Alfred W. *The Steam Locomotive in America*. New York: W. W. Norton & Co., 1952.

Forney, Matthias N. *Catechism of the Locomotive*. 1st ed. New York: Railroad Gazette, 1874.

Harrison, Joseph Jr. *The Locomotive and Philadelphia's Share in Its Early Improvements*. Philadelphia: Gebbie, 1872.

Ransome-Wallis, P. *The Concise Encyclopedia of World Railway Locomotives*. New York: Hawthorn, 1959.

Sinclair, Angus. *Development of the Locomotive Engine*. Annotated Edition. Cambridge: M. I. T. Press, 1970.

Swengel, F. M. *The American Steam Locomotive. Vol. 1 Evolution*. Davenport, Iowa: Midwest Rail Publications, Inc., 1967.

Westing, F. H. (ed.). *The Locomotives That Baldwin Built*. Seattle: Superior Publishing Co., 1966.

White, John H.. Jr. *American Locomotives: An Engineering History, 1830–1880*. Baltimore: Johns Hopkins Press, 1968.

In addition to the general works listed above, a large number of pictorial works have been published on the locomotives of individual railroads. Consult your local book dealer or library for details.

LIST OF PLATES

Part 1
Historical
Locomotives

1. Trevithick's first locomotive, Penn-y-Darran, Wales, 1804.
2. Blenkinsop's rack locomotive, Leeds, England, 1812.
3. Hedley's *Wylam Dilly, c.* 1814.
4. John Stevens' demonstration steam locomotive, Hoboken, 1825.
5. The *Stourbridge Lion,* first commercial locomotive in North America, 1829.
6. The *Pride of Newcastle,* built by Robert Stephenson and Co., 1828.
7. The *Liverpool,* built by Edward Bury of Liverpool, England, 1830.
8. Samson-class locomotive built by Robert Stephenson and Co. in 1830.
9. The *Herald,* Samson-class locomotive of the Baltimore and Susquehanna Railroad, 1831.
10. The *Best Friend,* West Point Foundry for the South Carolina Railroad, 1830.
11. The *West Point,* completed in 1831 for the South Carolina Railroad.
12. The *De Witt Clinton,* West Point Foundry for the Mohawk and Hudson Railroad, 1831.
13. Reconstruction of locomotive built by William T. James for the Baltimore and Ohio Railroad, 1831.
14. The *Experiment,* West Point Foundry for the Mohawk and Hudson Railroad, 1832.
15. A standard Norris locomotive of about 1840.
16. The *Sandusky,* first locomotive built by Thomas Rogers of Paterson, New Jersey, 1837.
17. Campbell's eight wheeler completed in 1837 for Philadelphia, Germantown and Norristown Railroad.
18. The *Hercules,* Eastwick and Harrison's improvement of Campbell's plan, 1836–1837.
19. The *Andrew Jackson,* Ross Winans' grasshopper, built in 1836 and remodeled in 1892 to represent the Atlantic.
20. The *Mazeppa,* an improvement of the grasshopper, known as the "crab," 1838.
21. The "mud digger," an eight-wheel version of the crab, built in 1841 and 1842.
22. The *Cumberland,* a more powerful form of mud digger Winans devised for the B & O, 1845.
23. Camden and Amboy's *John Stevens* based on an English design, 1849.
24. The *Illinois,* a high-speed express locomotive built in 1852 by James Millholland.

25. The *General*, built in 1855 by Rogers for the Western and Atlantic Railroad.

26. The *Phantom*, a wood-burning locomotive built in 1857 by William Mason, Taunton, Massachusetts.

27. Standard eight wheeler typical of its maker, the Rogers Locomotive and Machine Works, *c.* 1865.

28. The *Pennsylvania*, a heavy pusher engine built in 1863 by the Philadelphia and Reading Railroad.

29. The *Reuben Wells*, a ten-wheel tank engine, built for the Madison and Indianapolis Railroad in 1868.

30. The *Janus*, patterned on a British patent of R. F. Fairlie, built in 1869–1870 for the Central Pacific Railroad by Mason Machine Works.

31. The *Consolidation*, a new style of freight locomotive introduced by the Baldwin works in 1866.

32. The *Sampson*, a six-wheel tank locomotive built by Union Iron Works, San Francisco, 1867.

33. The *America*, built by Grant Locomotive Works of Paterson, New Jersey, for the Paris Exposition of 1867.

34. The *John B. Turner*, constructed in shops of the Chicago and North Western Railway in 1867.

35. The *General Darcy* and the *N. Perry*, built in shops of the New Jersey Railroad and Transportation Company in 1868 and 1867 respectively.

36. New Jersey Railroad and Transportation Co.'s *No. 44*, 1870.

37. New Jersey Railroad and Transportation Co.'s *No. 143*, 1870.

38. Pittsburgh, Fort Wayne and Chicago eight wheeler, *c.* 1869.

39. Boston and Albany's *242*, built by Wilson Eddy, 1874.

**Part 2
Main-Line
Locomotives**

40. Baldwin American, Baldwin Locomotive Works, Philadelphia, 1871.

41. Side elevation section of the Baldwin American, 1871.

42. Grant American, Grant Locomotive Works, Paterson, New Jersey, 1873.

43. Baldwin Mogul, Baldwin Locomotive Works, Philadelphia, 1872.

44. Baltimore and Ohio Railroad Mogul, *No. 600*, B & O Shops, Baltimore, 1875.

45. Boston, Concord and Montreal Railroad Mogul, *Mt. Washington*, Manchester Locomotive Works, Manchester, New Hampshire, 1879.

46. Philadelphia and Reading Railroad Consolidation, *No. 415*, Baldwin Locomotive Works, Philadelphia, 1880.

47. Pennsylvania Railroad Consolidation, *No. 400*, Pennsylvania Shops, Altoona, Pennsylvania, 1885.

48. Lehigh Valley Railroad, *No. 82*, *Bee*, Lancaster, Pennsylvania, 1867.

49. Lehigh Valley Railroad Twelve Wheeler, *Champion*, Lehigh Valley Shops, Weatherly, Pennsylvania, 1882.

50. Central Pacific Railroad Twelve Wheeler, *No. 229*, Central Pacific Shops, Sacramento, 1882.

51. Pennsylvania Railroad American, *No. 10*, Pennsylvania Shops, Altoona, Pennsylvania, 1881.

52. Philadelphia and Reading Railroad American, *No. 411*, P & R Shops, Reading, Pennsylvania, 1880.

53. St. Louis and San Francisco Railroad American, *Capt. C. W. Rogers*, Rogers Locomotive Works, Paterson, New Jersey, 1880.

54. Long Island Railroad American, *No. 83*, Rogers Locomotive Works, Paterson, New Jersey, 1882.

55. New York, Susquehanna and Western Railroad Mogul, *No. 35*, Rogers Locomotive Works, Paterson, New Jersey, 1884.

56. New York, New Haven and Hartford Railroad American, *No. 106*, New Haven Shops, New Haven, Connecticut, 1882.

57. Michigan Central Railroad Mogul, *No. 269*, Schenectady Locomotive Works, Schenectady, New York, 1886.

58. Ohio and Mississippi Railway American, *No. 53*, rebuilt at the O & M Shops, Vincennes, Indiana, 1888.

59. Pennsylvania Railroad American, *No. 1222*, Pennsylvania Shops, Altoona, Pennsylvania, 1888.

60. Lake Shore and Michigan Southern Railway American, *No. 220*, Brooks Locomotive Works, Dunkirk, New York, 1888.

61. Lake Shore and Michigan Southern Railway American, *No. 195*, Schenectady Locomotive Works, Schenectady, New York, 1886.

62. Chicago, Milwaukee and St. Paul Railroad, *No. 796*, Schenectady Locomotive Works, Schenectady, New York, 1889.

63. Northern Pacific Railroad Consolidation, *No. 10,000*, Baldwin Locomotive Works, Philadelphia, 1889.

64. Baltimore and Ohio Railroad American, *No. 859*, Baldwin Locmotive Works, Philadelphia, 1893.

65. New York, Lake Erie and Western Railway Decapod, *No. 805*, Baldwin Locomotive Works, Philadelphia, 1893.

66. Philadelphia and Reading Railroad Columbia, *No. 694*, Baldwin Locomotive Works, Philadelphia, 1893.

67. Baltimore and Ohio Railroad American, *No. 858*, Baldwin Locomotive Works, Philadelphia, 1893.
    Baltimore and Ohio Railroad American, *No. 887*, Baldwin Locomotive Works, Philadelphia, 1893.
    Baltimore and Ohio Railroad Consolidation, *No. 1223*, Baldwin Locomotive Works, Philadelphia, 1893.

68. Baltimore and Ohio Railroad Ten Wheeler, *No. 1342*, Baldwin Locomotive Works, Philadelphia, 1893.
    Central Railroad of New Jersey American, *No. 450*, Baldwin Locomotive Works, Philadelphia, 1893.
    Norfolk and Western Railroad Consolidation, *No. 330*, Baldwin Locomotive Works, Philadelphia, 1893.

69. Baltimore and Ohio South Western Railway Ten Wheeler, *No. 123*, Baldwin Locomotive Works, Philadelphia, 1893.

70. Lima Northern Railroad Mogul, *No. 61*, Baldwin Locomotive Works, Philadelphia, 1893.

71. Lake Shore and Michigan Southern Railway Ten Wheeler, *No. 600*, Brooks Locomotive Works, Dunkirk, New York, 1893.

72. Cincinnati, Hamilton and Dayton Railroad American, *No. 210*, Brooks Locomotive Works, Dunkirk, New York, 1893.

73. Great Northern Railway Mastodon, *No. 410*, Brooks Locomotive Works, Dunkirk, New York, 1893.

74. Great Northern Railway Consolidation, *No. 515*, Brooks Locomotive Works, Dunkirk, New York, 1893.

75. Lake Shore and Michigan Southern Railway American, *No. 599*, Brooks Locomotive Works, Dunkirk, New York, 1893.

76. Great Northern Railway Ten Wheeler, *No. 650*, Brooks Locomotive Works, Dunkirk, New York, 1893.

77. Great Northern Railway Mogul, *No. 351*, Brooks Locomotive Works, Dunkirk, New York, 1893.

78. Canadian Pacific Railway Ten Wheeler, *No. 626*, Canadian Pacific Shops, Montreal, 1893.

79. New York Central and Hudson River Railroad American, *No. 999*, 1892.

80. Old Colony Railroad American, *No. 256*, Old Colony Shops, Boston, 1893.

81. Terre Haute and Indianapolis Railroad (Vandalia Line) Ten Wheeler, *No. 1450*, Pittsburg Locomotive Works, Pittsburg, 1893.

82. Chicago, Milwaukee and St. Paul Railway Pacific, *No. 830*, Rhode Island Locomotive Works, Providence, 1893.

83. New York, New Haven and Hartford Railroad American, *No. 254*, Rhode Island Locomotive Works, Providence, 1893.

84. Minneapolis, St. Paul and Sault Ste. Marie Railroad (Soo Line) Consolidation, *No. 400*, Rhode Island Locomotive Works, Providence, 1893.

85. Chesapeake and Ohio Railroad Consolidation, *No. 350*, Richmond Locomotive Works, Richmond, 1893.

86. Chicago, Burlington and Quincy Railroad American, *No. 550*, Rogers Locomotive Works, Paterson, New Jersey, 1893.

87. Charleston and Savannah Railway (Plant System) Ten Wheeler, *No. 100*, Rogers Locomotive Works, Paterson, New Jersey, 1893.

88. Chicago and North Western Railway Ten Wheeler, *No. 400*, Schenectady Locomotive Works, Schenectady, New York, 1893.

89. Duluth and Iron Range Railroad Twelve Wheeler, *No. 60*, Schenectady Locomotive Works, Schenectady, New York, 1893.

90. Mohawk and Malone Railroad Consolidation, *No. 61*, Schenectady Locomotive Works, Schenectady, New York, 1893.

Part 3
Special Service

91. Canada Southern Railroad Fontaine Locomotive, Grant Locomotive Works, Paterson, New Jersey, 1881.

92. Philadelphia and Reading Railroad (Bound Brook Line), *No. 507*, Baldwin Locomotive Works, Philadelphia, 1880.

93. Central Pacific Railroad Prairie Tank Locomotive, *No. 236*, Central Pacific Shops, Sacramento, California, 1882.

94. Atchison, Topeka and Santa Fe Railroad Consolidation, *Uncle Dick*, Baldwin Locomotive Works, Philadelphia, 1878.

95. Billerica and Bedford Railroad Forney, *Ariel*, Hinkley Locomotive Works, Boston, 1877.

96. New York Elevated Railroad Forney, *No. 39*, Baldwin Locomotive Works, Philadelphia, 1878.

97. New York and Harlem Railroad Forney, *No. 26*, Schenectady Locomotive Works, Schenectady, New York, 1876.

98. Denver, South Park and Pacific Railroad Mason double truck, *Breckenridge,* Mason Machine Works, Taunton, Massachusetts, 1879.

99. Providence, Warren and Bristol Railroad Mason double truck, *Pokanoket,* Mason Machine Works, Taunton, Massachusetts, 1885.

100. Providence, Warren and Bristol Railroad, *Annawomscutt,* Taunton Locomotive Manufacturing Company, Taunton, Massachusetts, 1887.

101. Forney locomotive for unknown railroad, Brooks Locomotive Works, Dunkirk, New York, *c.* 1885.

102. Indianapolis and Evansville Railway Forney, Rhode Island Locomotive Works, Providence, 1880.

103. Saginaw Bay and North Western Railroad 0–4–2, *John C. Durgin,* H. K. Porter and Co., Pittsburgh, 1884.

104. Central Railroad of New Jersey, *No. 196,* Grant Locomotive Works, Paterson, New Jersey, 1872.

105. Illinois Central Railroad Ten Wheel Double-Ender, *No. 213,* Rogers Locomotive Works, Paterson, New Jersey, 1880.

106. Longfellow Mining Co. (Arizona) 0–4–0T, *Coronada,* H. K. Porter and Co., Pittsburg, 1880.

107. Steel mill service 0–4–0T, Pittsburg Locomotive Works, Pittsburg, 1893.

108. New Mexico Railway and Coal Co. 2–4–2T, *No. 13361,* Baldwin Locomotive Works, Philadelphia, 1893.

109. Mine locomotive 0–4–0, Dickson Manufacturing Co., Scranton, Pennsylvania, *c.* 1885.

110. Baltimore and Potomac Railroad, *No. 22,* Baldwin Locomotive Works, Philadelphia, 1873.

111. Prince of Grand Pará Railroad (Brazil) rack locomotive, *Gurjao,* Baldwin Locomotive Works, Philadelphia, 1886.

112. Pole road locomotive, *Perdido,* Adams and Price, Nashville, 1884.

113. Hardwick and Woodbury Railroad Shay geared locomotive, *No. 450,* Lima Locomotive Works, Lima, Ohio, 1893.

114. Haydenville Branch Railroad 0–4–0, *No. 2,* Rogers Locomotive Works, Paterson, New Jersey, 1879.

115. 0–4–0, *No. 11,* Cooke Locomotive and Machine Works, Paterson, New Jersey, *c.* 1885.

116. Georgia Railroad, *No. 21,* Rogers Locomotive Works, Paterson, New Jersey, 1877.

117. Chicago and North Western Railway, *No. 140,* Schenectady Locomotive Works, Schenectady, New York, 1893.

118. Great Northern Railway, *No. 258,* Brooks Locomotive Works, Dunkirk, New York, 1893.

119. Crescent City Railway (New Orleans) fireless locomotive, Theodore Scheffler, Paterson, New Jersey, 1876.

120. Central Railroad of New Jersey, *Star,* C.R.R.N.J. shops, Elizabethport, New Jersey, 1871.

Part 4
Export and
Foreign

121. London and North Western Railway, *No. 503*, Francis W. Webb, Crewe, England, 1884.

122. London and North Western Railway, *No. 1301*, London and North Western Shops, Crewe, England, 1889.

123. London and North Western Railway, *Cornwall*, 1847, and *Nipper.*

124. Great Northern Railway (England), *No. 232*, Great Northern Shops, Doncaster, England, 1885.

125. Caledonian Railway 4–4–0, *No. 128*, Neilson and Co., Glasgow, Scotland, *c.* 1881.

126. Southeastern Railway six-wheel goods engine, *No. 285*, Sharp, Stewart and Co., Manchester, England, *c.* 1882.

127. London, Brighton and South Coast Railway Terrier, *Brighton, c.* 1882.

128. Northeastern Railway, *No. 947*, Neilson and Co., Glasgow, Scotland, 1874.

129. Great Southern and Western Railway of Ireland, *No. 35*, Great Southern and Western Shops, 1879.

130. Mersey River Tunnel Railway, *No. 1*, Beyer, Peacock and Co., Manchester, England, 1886.

131. Experimental locomotive, *James Toleman*, Hawthorne, Leslie and Co., Newcastle, England, 1892.

132. Western Railway of France, *No. 3535*, Compagnie de Fives-Lille, *c.* 1885.

133. Wurtemburg State Railroad 2–4–0, Esslingen Machine Works, Esslingen, Germany, *c.* 1875.

134. Swiss Northeastern Railroad 0–4–0, *No. 98*, Esslingen Machine Works, Esslingen, Germany, 1874.

135. Swiss compensating lever locomotive, Swiss Locomotive Works, Winterthur, Switzerland, 1878.

136. Villa Real and Villa Regoa Tramway (Portugal) 0–6–0–0–6–0, Swiss Locomotive Works, Winterthur, Switzerland, *c.* 1878.

137. New Zealand Railway Columbia, *Washington*, Rogers Locomotive Works, Paterson, New Jersey, 1877.

138. New Zealand Railway Prairie, Baldwin Locomotive Works, Philadelphia, 1885.

139. Mejía and Arequipa Railway (Peru) steam inspection car, *La Joya*, Rogers Locomotive Works, Paterson, New Jersey, 1869.

140. Paulista Railroad (Brazil) Consolidation, *No. 17*, Dubs and Co., Glasgow, Scotland, 1884.

141. Dom Pedro II Railroad (Brazil) Decapod, Baldwin Locomotive Works, Philadelphia, 1885.

142. Mejía and Arequipa Railway (Peru) Mogul, *No. 750*, Danforth, Cooke and Company, Paterson, New Jersey, 1871.

143. Nuevitas and Puerto Príncipe Railway (Cuba) Ten Wheeler, *No. 7*, Rogers Locomotive Works, Paterson, New Jersey, 1874.

144. Leopoldina Railway (Brazil) Mogul, *Antonio Carlos*, Rogers Locomotive Works, Paterson, New Jersey, 1878.

145. Barão de Araucana Railway (Brazil) Mogul, *Santa Maria Magdalena*, Rogers Locomotive Works, Paterson, New Jersey, 1878.

146. *Desempeño*, Rogers Locomotive Works, Paterson, New Jersey, 1875.

147. Matanzas Railroad (Cuba), *No. 32*, Rogers Locomotive Works, Paterson, New Jersey, 1878.

LIST OF SOURCES FOR PLATES

Artizan, 1859.

Colburn, Zehra. *Locomotive Engineering.* London: W. Collins Sons, 1872.

Dredge, James. *A Record of the Transportation Exhibits at the World's Columbian Exposition of 1893.*

Engineer, 1879.

Engineering, 1867–1871.

Forney, Matthias N. *Catechism of the Locomotive.* New York: Railroad Gazette, 1874 and 1890.

Forney, Matthias N. *Locomotives and Locomotive Building.* . . . New York, 1886. (*Rogers Catalog*).

(Forney, Matthias N.) *Recent Locomotives: Illustrations, with Descriptions and Specifications and Details, of Recent American and European Locomotives, Reprinted from the Railroad Gazette.* . . . New York: *The Railroad Gazette,* 1886.

Harrison, Joseph. *The Locomotive Engine.* Philadelphia: G. Gebbie, 1872.

Locomotive Engineering, 1891.

Railroad Gazette, 1882–1889.

Renwick James. *Treatise on the Steam Engine.* New York: G., C. and H. Carvill, 1830.

Scientific American and *Scientific American Supplement,* 1869–1897.

Weissenborn, G. *American Locomotive Engineering and Railway Mechanism: With a Practical Treatise on the Construction and Principles of the Locomotive Engine and Railway Cars.* New York: The American Industrial Publishing Co., 1871.

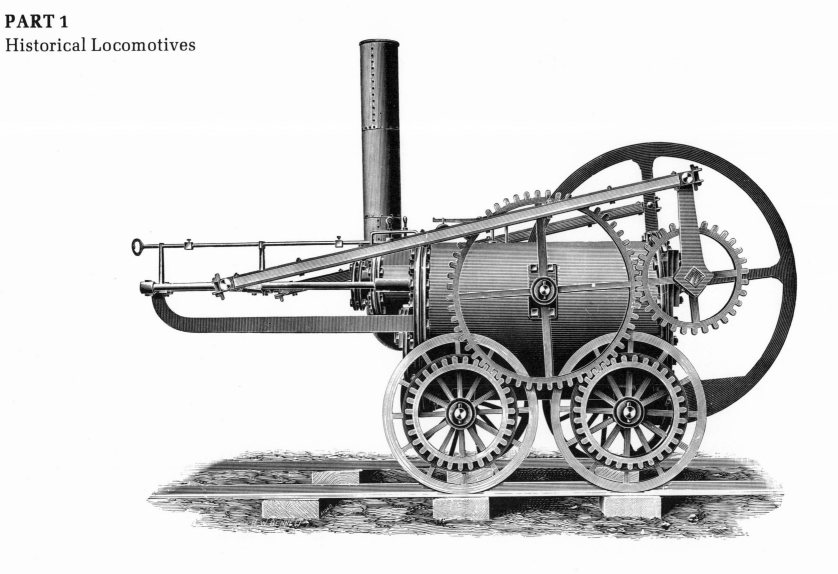

1 In 1804 Richard Trevithick built the first railway locomotive. The machine was actually an adaptation of its maker's portable engine. It operated for a short time on the tramway of the Penn-y-Darran Iron Works in southern Wales. (*Dredge*, Plate LXXXVIII, Fig. 1)

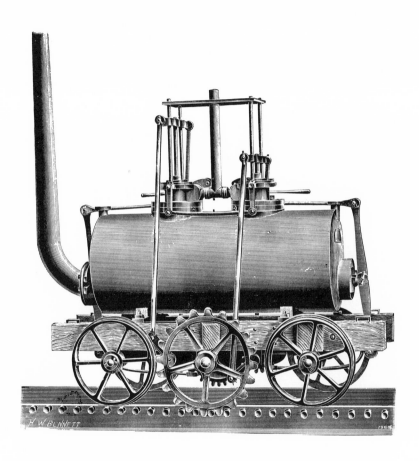

2 John Blenkinsop of Leeds, England devised this rack locomotive some eight years after Trevithick's first attempt at steam locomotion. It proved a reasonably successful design. Several were built and all saw long service on the Middleton Colliery's tramway. (*Dredge*, Plate LXXXIV, Fig. 1)

3 Other coal-mine mechanics were inspired by Blenkinsop's success, and soon many "fiery chariots" were traversing Britain's tramways. Clumsy and slow moving, they were nevertheless considered wonders of the age. This example is the *Wylam Dilly* built in about 1814 by William Hedley. (*Dredge*, Plate LXXXIV, Fig. 2)

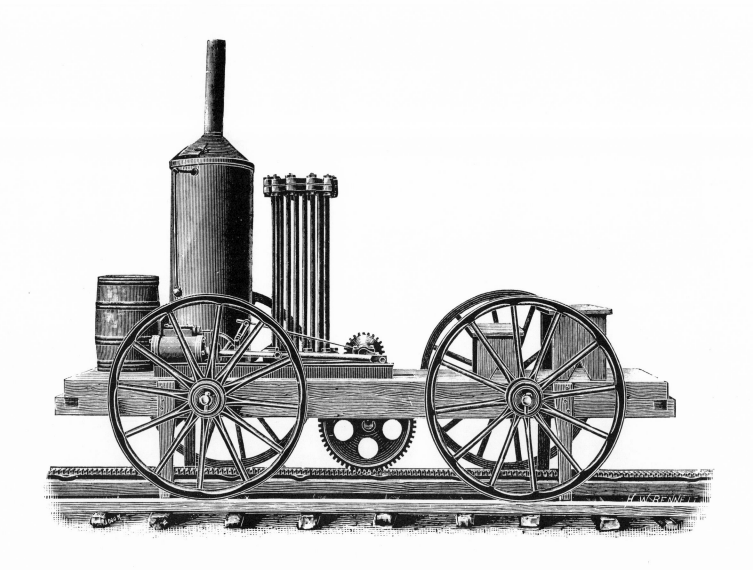

4 John Stevens of Hoboken, New Jersey, advocated railways as the best means of transport for tapping the riches of America's inland empire. To dramatize the practicability of steam locomotion, he built this demonstration locomotive in 1825 for a circular railway on his estate. In the drawing the boiler tube unit is shown outside the vertical boiler shell, which is at the rear of the machine. (*Dredge*, Plate XC, Fig. 1)

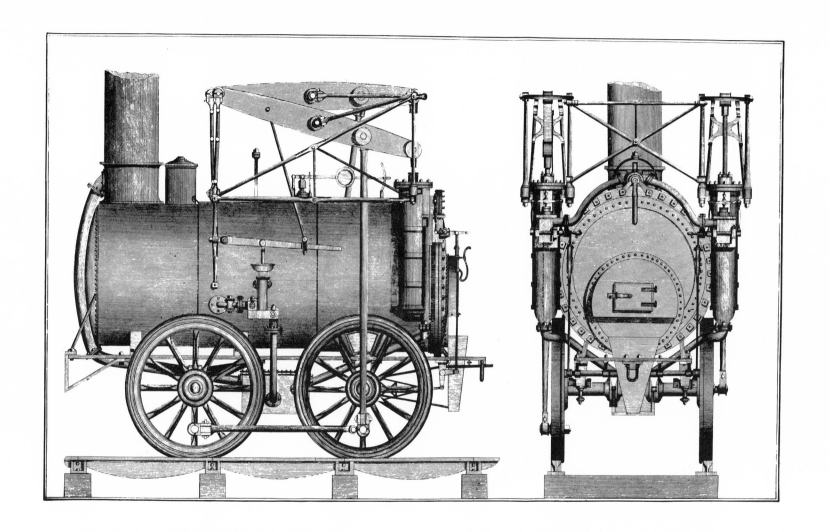

5 The first commercial locomotive to turn a wheel in North America was imported from England by the Delaware and Hudson Canal Company in 1829 for a short coal railroad in northeastern Pennsylvania. The *Stourbridge Lion* proved too heavy for the light tracks and was retired after a few test runs. Relics of this historic machine are exhibited by the Smithsonian Institution. (James Renwick, *The Steam Engine...*, 1830, Plate IX)

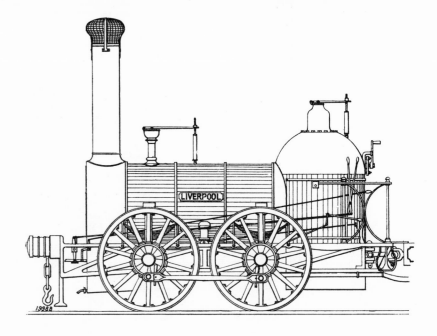

6 Another locomotive imported at the same time by the D & H Canal Company is shown in this engraving. The actual name is now believed to have been *Pride of Newcastle* rather than *America*. This engine was built by Robert Stephenson and Company in 1828. Like the *Stourbridge Lion* it saw no actual service. (*Dredge*, Plate LXXXIV, Fig. 5)

7 The *Liverpool* was built by Edward Bury of Liverpool, England, in 1830. After several misadventures and reconstructions it was exported to the United States for service on the Petersburg Railroad in Virginia. Bury was a major builder of locomotives for the American market during the short period in which this country sought locomotives abroad. (*Dredge*, Plate LXXXV, Fig. 2)

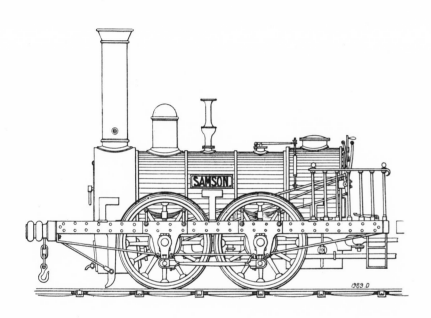

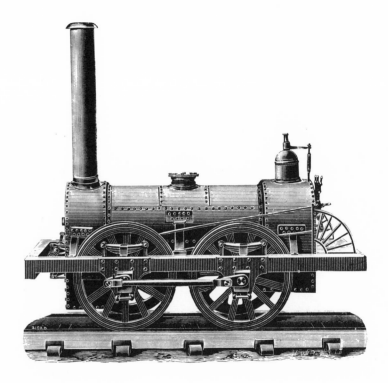

8 A favorite model of Robert Stephenson and Company was the four-wheel, inside cylinder, Samson class. The original machine of that design was built in 1830 for the Liverpool and Manchester Railway. A number of Samsons were used on railways in this country. (*Dredge,* LXXXV, Fig. 5)

9 The *Herald* is an example of a Samson-class machine that saw service in this country. The Baltimore and Susquehanna Railroad was not satisfied with the performance of the typically rigid British locomotive. The four-wheel leading truck which replaced the front driving wheels did much to improve the *Herald's* operation. A second rebuilding some years later transformed the aging import into a six-wheel, geared switcher. Originally built in 1831, the *Herald* was retired in about 1859. (*Dredge,* Plate XC, Fig. 2)

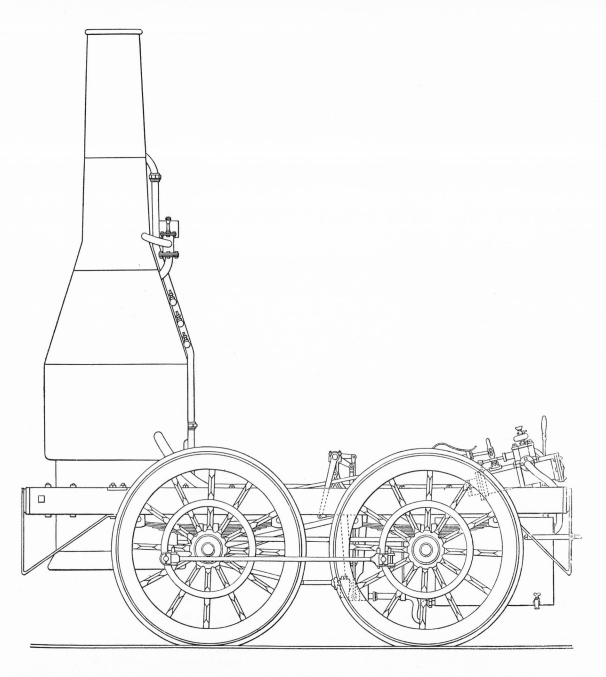

10 The railway era had hardly started in America before native mechanics began the fabrication of locomotives. The *Best Friend* was the first. She was built in 1830 for the South Carolina Railroad by the West Point Foundry in New York City. (*Railroad Gazette,* May 25, 1883, p. 324)

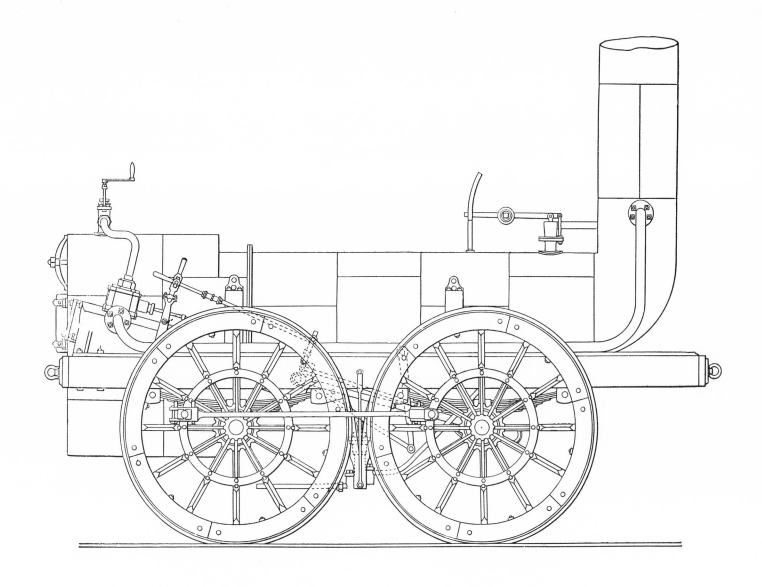

11 Another product of the pioneer West Point Foundry was the locomotive *West Point*. It was completed in 1831 for the South Carolina Railroad and saw less than seven years' service. This engraving, like the illustration of the *Best Friend*, was based on an original drawing. (*Railroad Gazette*, May 25, 1883, p. 325)

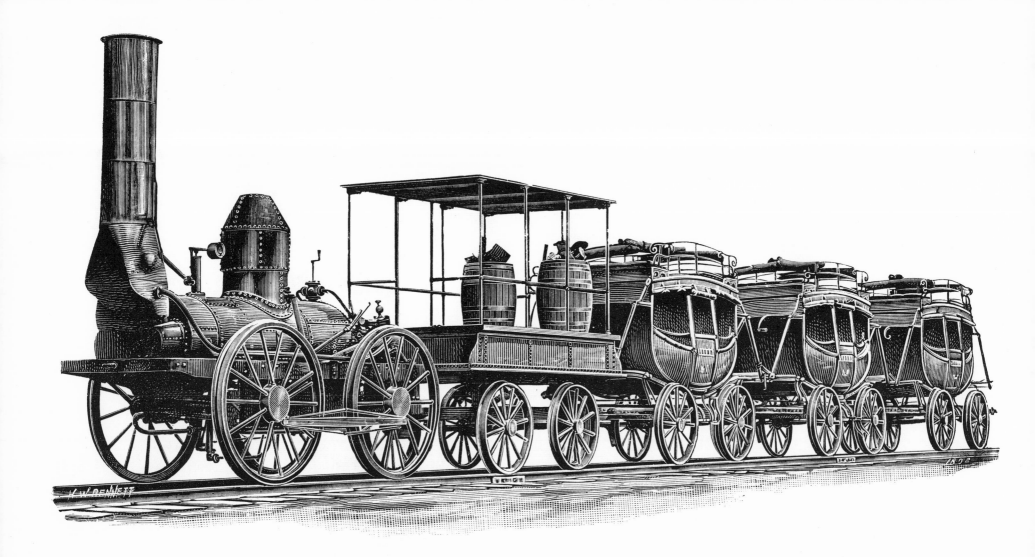

12 Similar in its general arrangement, the *De Witt Clinton* was built in the same year as the *West Point*. Also a product of the West Point Foundry, the *Clinton* was the first locomotive on the Mohawk and Hudson Railroad. The engraving shown here is after the replica built by the New York Central for the 1893 Chicago Exposition. The replica stands today in the Ford Museum. The original was retired after one year's service. (*Dredge*, Plate LXXXII, Fig. 2)

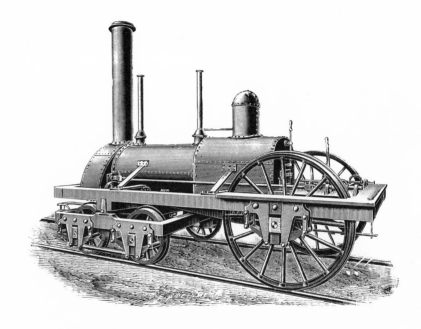

13 William T. James operated a stove foundry in New York during the years the West Point works began locomotive production. It was his wish to enter the field as well. Several machines were built in the 1830's and while many exhibited some novel mechanical idea, James was not destined to become a major figure in the railway supply trade. The drawing shown here is of a reconstruction of a locomotive made in 1893 for the Baltimore and Ohio Railroad. (*Dredge*, Plate LXXXI, Fig. 1)

14 The *Experiment*, built by the West Point Foundry, was the first locomotive to employ a leading truck. The small front wheels guided locomotives over the rough tracks of America's early railroads. This major improvement was introduced in 1832 by John B. Jervis, then chief engineer for the Mohawk and Hudson Railroad. The *Experiment* was renamed the *Brother Jonathan*. It was later converted to an eight-wheel locomotive and continued in service for many years. (*Dredge*, Plate LXXXI, Fig. 2)

15 This engraving purports to represent the *George Washington.* The remarkable performance of this machine in surmounting the Belmont incline on the Philadelphia and Columbia Railroad in 1836 won an international reputation for its maker, William Norris of Philadelphia. However, contemporary evidence shows that the original machine differed in several important mechanical details, notably inside cylinders. The engraving does accurately portray a standard Norris locomotive of about 1840. (*Dredge,* Plate XC, Fig. 3)

16 The Mad River and Lake Erie Railroad's *Sandusky* was one of the first locomotives shipped west of the Alleghenies. It was also the first locomotive built by Thomas Rogers of Paterson, New Jersey (1837). Rogers was a major locomotive maker in the nineteenth century. (*Dredge,* Plate LXXXVII, Fig. 4)

17 In 1836 Henry R. Campbell of Philadelphia devised a powerful and wonderfully flexible locomotive by adding an extra pair of driving wheels to Jervis's truck engine, examples of which have been shown in the three previous illustrations. The first Campbell eight wheeler was completed in 1837 for the Philadelphia, Germantown and Norristown Railroad, now a part of the Reading. (*Dredge*, Plate LXXXI, Fig. 3)

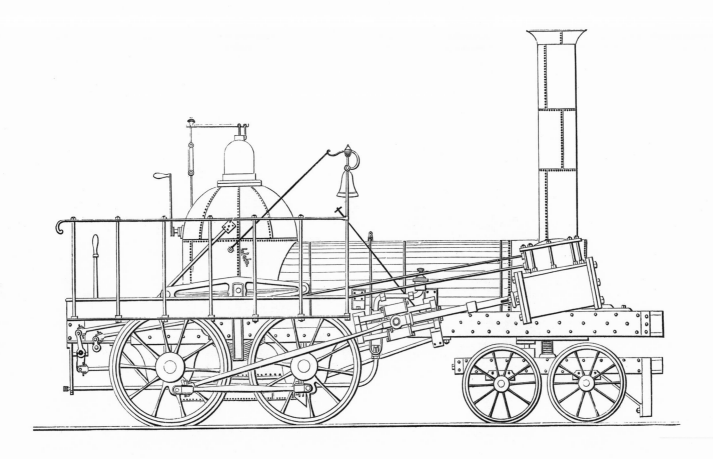

18 Campbell's plan was materially improved by Eastwick and Harrison, also of Philadelphia, whose subsequent running gear modification made the eight-wheel truck locomotive a national standard. This style of locomotive was to remain a universal favorite in this country until late in the century. The *Hercules* was completed 1836–1837 for the Beaver Meadow Railroad. In the drawing it is shown after being fitted with Harrison's patented equalizing lever. (Joseph Harrison, *The Locomotive Engine...*, 1872, opp. p. 49)

19 While the truck locomotive was the mainstream of American development, Ross Winans of Baltimore pursued an independent course that led to the curious designs that are shown in the following several illustrations. At first Winans continued with his predecessor's grasshopper design, as shown by this engraving of the *Andrew Jackson* (1832). It was remodeled in 1892 to represent the *Atlantic* (1832) and stands today in its altered form in the B & O Museum, Baltimore. (*Railroad Gazette*, Aug. 10, 1883, p. 521)

20 Winans improved the grasshopper plan by using horizontal cylinders. The new design became popularly known as the "crab" engine. One of them, named most inappropriately for Byron's poem, *Mazeppa*, was built in 1838. The engraving here is after a partial replica built for the 1893 Exposition. (*Dredge*, Plate LXXXI, Fig. 5)

21 The "mud digger" was an eight-wheel version of the crab. A number were built in 1841 and 1842 for the Western Railroad (Massachusetts). They were not considered entirely satisfactory and all were retired by 1850. (*Dredge*, Plate LXXXI, Fig. 6)

22 The *Cumberland* was a more powerful form of mud digger which Winans devised for the B & O. Built in 1845 and later known simply as *No. 37*, the machine continued in service until the late 1860's. (*Engineer*, Jan. 24, 1879, p. 68)

23 Winans had no monopoly on novel designs. Other mavericks such as the Camden and Amboy Railroad's *John Stevens* roamed the tracks. Several sister locomotives based on the same English design were built between 1849 and 1853. All were remodeled on more conventional lines after a few years' service. (*Scientific American Supplement,* May 8, 1897, p. 17807)

24 A somewhat more orthodox attempt at developing a high-speed
express locomotive was James Millholland's *Illinois*. Built in 1852
for the Philadelphia and Reading, her high wheels permitted fast
running but the peculiar coal-burning boiler was a failure and only
one other engine was made on the same design. (*Railroad Gazette*,
Oct. 27, 1882, p. 655)

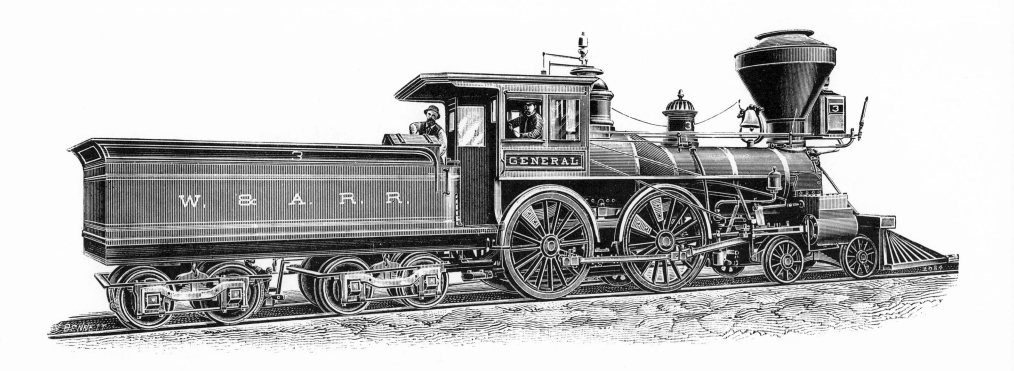

25 The *General*, perhaps the most famous locomotive in American history, was involved in one of the most exciting adventures of the Civil War. She was built in 1855 by Rogers for the Western and Atlantic Railroad. For many years the *General* was exhibited in Chattanooga. It is now scheduled for exhibit near Atlanta. (*Dredge*, Plate LXXXIII, Fig. 2)

26 The *Phantom* was built in 1857 by William Mason of Taunton, Massachusetts, a builder noted for his handsome locomotives. This wood-burning, straight-boilered eight wheeler saw service on the Toledo and Illinois Railroad. (*Artizan*, Feb. 1, 1859, Plate 138)

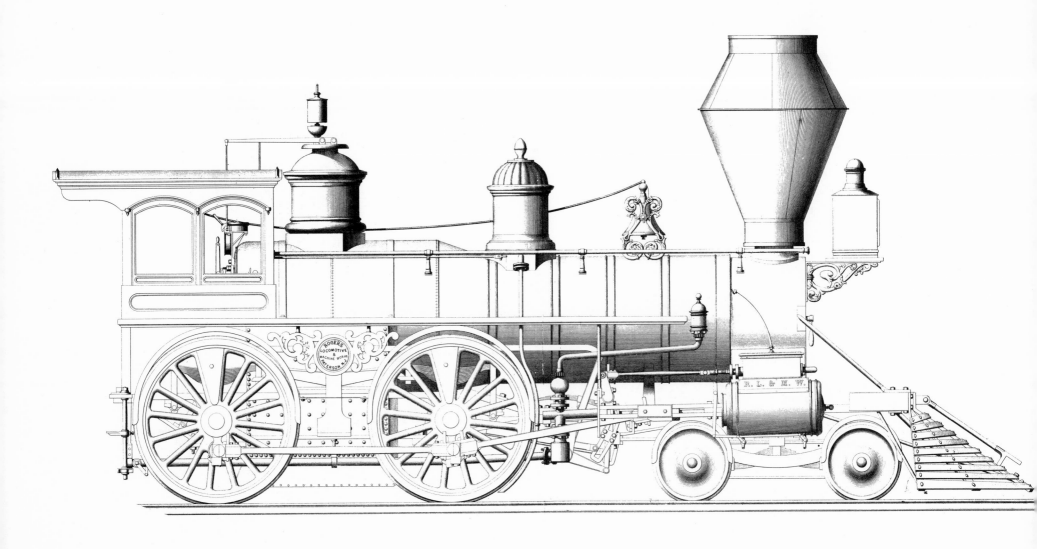

27 This standard eight wheeler cannot be precisely identified, but it is a typical product of the Rogers Locomotive and Machine Works. Built in about 1865, it is representative of machines that were used for all classes of service in that era. (Z. Colburn, *Locomotive Engineering...*, 1872, Plate XVIII)

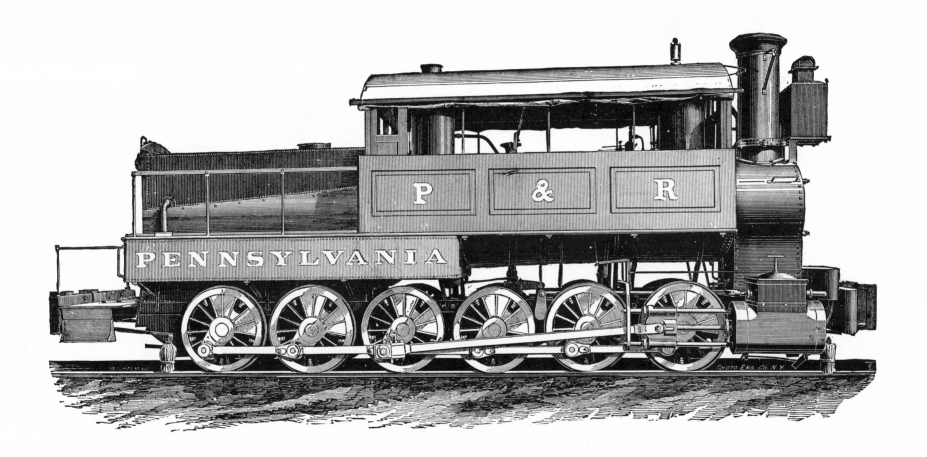

28 In the following three illustrations examples are shown of extra-heavy pusher engines. These ponderous machines were designed expressly to help trains up steep grades. The *Pennsyl-* *vania* was built in 1863 at the Philadelphia and Reading Railroad's repair shops. Weighing 50 tons, it was for a time the largest locomotive in the world. (*Recent Locomotives*, Fig. 80)

29 Five years after the *Pennsylvania* entered service, an even heavier locomotive was built far to the west for service on the Madison, Indiana, incline, the steepest standard-gauge grade in this country. The mammoth ten-wheel tank engine was named for its designer, Reuben Wells, master mechanic of the Jeffersonville, Madison and Indianapolis Railroad. It is exhibited today in the Children's Museum, Indianapolis, Indiana. (*Engineering*, Feb. 12, 1869, p. 108)

30 Based on a British patent of R. F. Fairlie, the *Janus* was built in 1869–1870 for the Central Pacific Railroad by the Mason Machine Works. It was not accepted by the Central Pacific and ended its days on the Lehigh Valley Railroad. A single bogie design was offered by Mason but no more double-ended Fairlies were built in this country. (*Scientific American*, Sept. 4, 1869, p. 148)

31 At the time these ponderous pusher engines were being built, the Baldwin Works of Philadelphia introduced a new style of freight locomotive which offered great capacity coupled with reasonably fast running speed. The *Consolidation* was completed in 1866 for the Lehigh Valley Railroad. This wheel arrangement soon became one of the most popular on our railroads. Several examples are shown elsewhere in this volume. (*Engineering*, Aug. 27, 1869, p. 146)

32 The Far West had several small locomotive builders. The most important was the Union Iron Works of San Francisco which built this six-wheel tank locomotive for the Pittsburgh Railroad in 1867. The four-wheel car to the rear of the engine is a coal hopper car, not a tender. (*Engineering,* Feb. 17, 1871, p. 115)

33 The Grant Locomotive Works of Paterson, New Jersey, built an elegantly finished locomotive for the Paris Exposition of 1867. It was covered with nickel silver and silver plated fittings; the cab was of rare cabinet wood. Mechanically it was conventional but its decor caught the fancy of the crowd and it was awarded a gold medal. The *America* was sold to the Chicago, Rock Island and Pacific Railroad after the Exposition closed. (*Engineering*, July 26, 1867, p. 64)

34 Most locomotives were products of commercial manufacturers but some railroads built at least a portion of their own rolling stock, as shown in the final illustrations in this part. The *John B. Turner* was constructed in the shops of the Chicago and North Western Railway in 1867. It remained in service until 1898. (*Engineering*, Nov. 20, 1868)

35 The *General Darcy* was a coal-burning freight locomotive built in the New Jersey Railroad and Transportation Company's Jersey City shops in 1868. Sold in 1881, its final disposition is unknown. The *N. Perry* was built in the same shops in 1867 and was sold in 1876. (*Engineering*, Oct. 16, 1868, opp. p. 294)

36 The New Jersey Railroad and Transportation Company is now an important segment of the Penn Central's main line between New York and Philadelphia. This company, in earlier years, built a number of locomotives in its Jersey City, New Jersey, shops. Among them was the 31-ton *No. 44* which was completed in October, 1870. Its ornate details suggest a design of the decade before. (*Weissenborn*, Plate 0)

37 Another product of the Jersey City shops was the coal-burning *No. 143*. It too was completed in 1870. Its builder, John Headden, succeeded William S. Hudson as superintendent of the Rogers Locomotive Works in 1881. (*Weissenborn*, Plate XVI)

38 This company-built eight wheeler was typical of the mixed-service engines produced by the Fort Wayne Shops in the late 1860's. This drawing agrees closely with the Pittsburgh, Fort Wayne & Chicago's *No. 199* which was completed in 1869, the same year the line was leased by the Pennsylvania Railroad. An interesting feature of this machine is the wood blocks inserted around the periphery of the driving wheels; these were meant to cushion and thereby extend the life of the soft wrought-iron tires. (*Weissenborn*, Plate XXII)

39 Wilson Eddy began building locomotives in the Springfield, Massachusetts, shops of the Western Railroad in the early 1850's. Their smooth-running precision earned them the title of "Eddy Clocks." The Boston and Albany's *242*, originally named the *Crocker*, was a late example of Eddy's production. Completed in 1874, it embodied many elements of Eddy's earliest design. (*Locomotive Engineering*, March 1891, p. 41)

40 A good representative locomotive for the period 1865–1885 is Baldwin's standard eight wheeler shown here. A typical design dated 1871, it cannot be assigned to any one locomotive. (*Recent Locomotives*, Fig. 1)

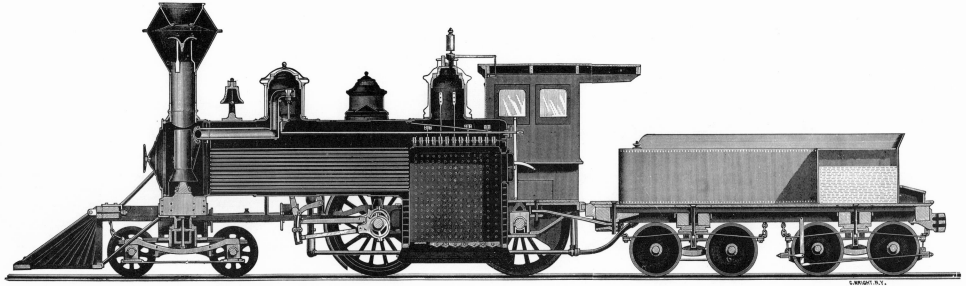

41 Here is the internal arrangement of the standard Baldwin locomotive shown in the preceding illustration. (*Recent Locomotives*, Figs. 2 & 3)

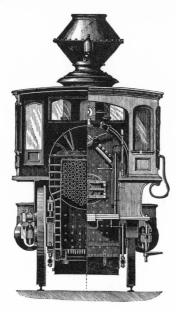

42 Similar to Baldwin's design was this 1873 offering of the Grant Locomotive Works. The small circular panels below the cab windows were intended to hold reproductions of the Gold Medal won by Grant at the 1867 Paris Exposition. The prize-winning entry is shown in Fig. 33. (*Recent Locomotives,* Figs. 4–6)

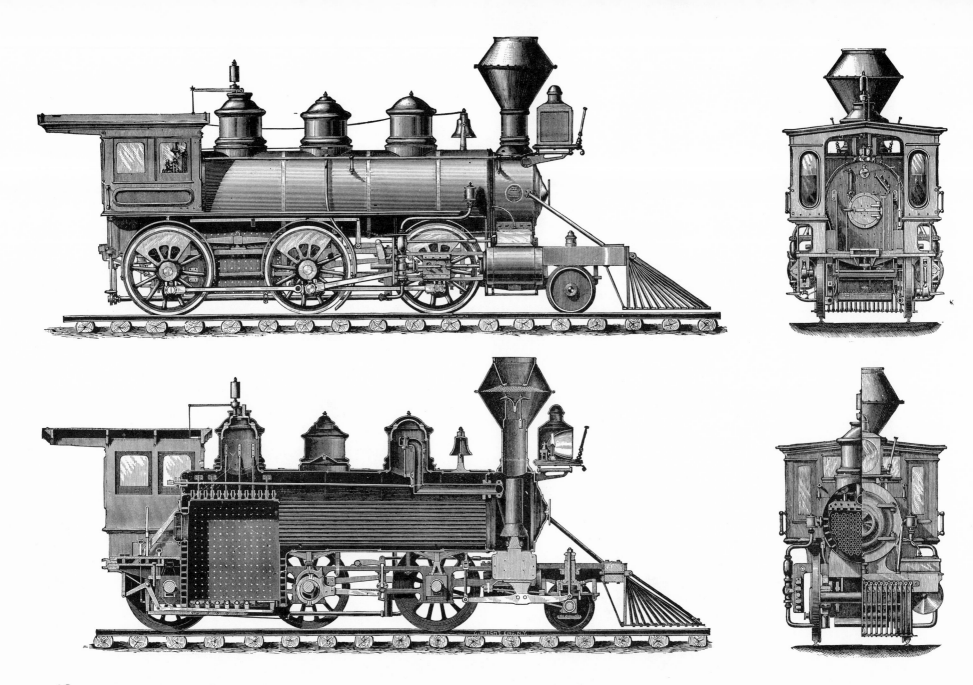

43 Baldwin offered this Mogul locomotive in 1872. Like the eight wheeler, it had a straight boiler with two steam domes. The relatively large wheels (54½ inches in diameter) indicate that the machine was designed for both freight and passenger service. (*Recent Locomotives*, Figs. 49–52)

44 The Baltimore and Ohio designed its Mogul *No. 600* specifically for passenger service. It was assigned to pull passenger trains over the steep Appalachian grades of West Virginia. Constructed in the B & O's Mt. Clare Shops (Baltimore) in 1875, it is now exhibited in a portion of these same workshops set aside as a railway museum. (*Recent Locomotives*, Fig. 54)

45 Another handsome Mogul was the Boston, Concord and Montreal's *Mt. Washington*. It was built in 1879 by the Manchester Locomotive Works (Manchester, New Hampire) and continued in service until 1907. The maker's workshops appear in the background of this engraving. (*Recent Locomotives*, Fig. 53)

46 This hard-coal-burning Consolidation freight locomotive was built in 1880 for the Philadelphia and Reading by Baldwin. Locomotives like the *415* with cabs atop the central portion of the boiler were often called "camel backs" or "Mother Hubbards." (*Recent Locomotives*, Fig. 70)

47 A more conventional-looking Consolidation was the Pennsylvania Railroad's *No. 400*. It was the first of the Class R series and was completed at the railroad's own Altoona, Pennsylvania, shops in October 1885. (*Recent Locomotives,* Fig. 309)

48 The *Bee* is shown here as it was rebuilt in 1883, with eight driving wheels and leading and trailing wheels. Originally it had ten drivers and a leading truck. The reconstruction was to assist backward movement. It was built in 1867 at Lancaster, Pennsylvania. (*Recent Locomotives*, Fig. 354)

49 Another wheel arrangement unusual for its time was to be found on the Lehigh Valley Railroad's *Champion*, completed in 1882 at the railroad's repair shops in Weatherly, Pennsylvania. (*Recent Locomotives,* Fig. 72)

50 In Sacramento, California, Andrew J. Stevens, the Central Pacific's master mechanic, put into practice his own special views on locomotive design. The *229* embodied many of his pet ideas. It was completed at the Sacramento shops in 1882 and saw over fifty years of service. (*Recent Locomotives,* Fig. 76)

51 The Pennsylvania's Class K was among the fastest express locomotives operating in this country during the 1880's. *Number 10,* the prototype, was built at Altoona in 1881. It was considered a remarkably advanced design at the time of its introduction. (*Recent Locomotives,* Fig. 22)

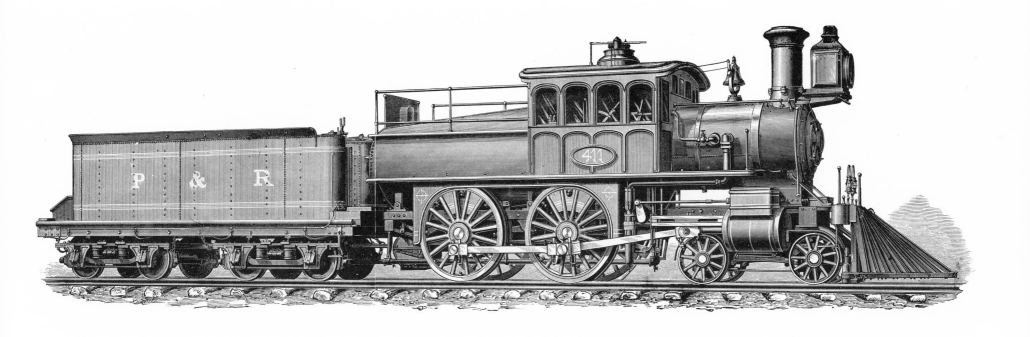

52 The Reading shops delivered this hard-coal burner in 1880. Like other Philadelphia and Reading locomotives of the day it was fitted with an extremely wide firebox patented by John E. Wootten, an official of the line. Wootten's firebox was eventually used by most other anthracite lines but saw little service outside of the Middle Atlantic states. The *411* was retired in 1907. (*Recent Locomotives,* Fig. 18)

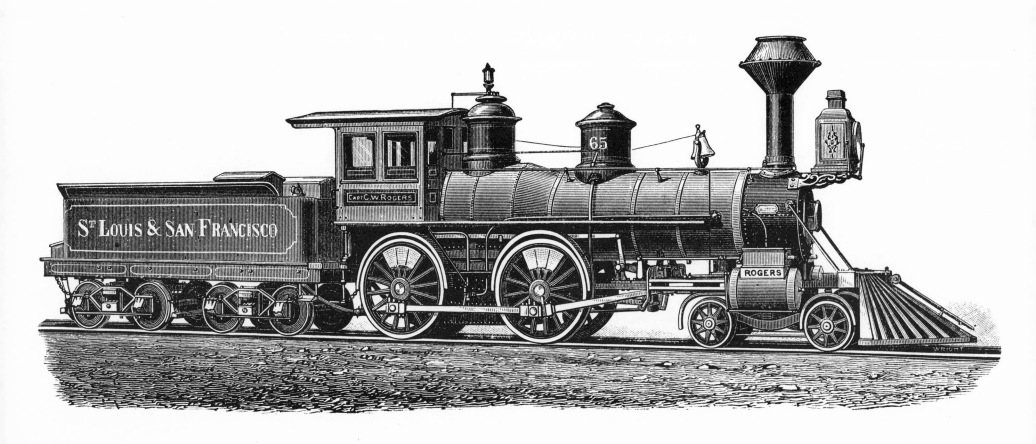

53 There is nothing exceptional about the *Capt. C. W. Rogers*. Rogers produced this simple, neat eight wheeler in August 1880 for the St. Louis and San Francisco Railroad. It was cut up in April, 1914. (*Rogers Catalog*, p. 102)

54 Somewhat more exotic than the previous Rogers product was the Long Island Railroad's *No. 83*, built in 1882. An anthracite burner, its appearance was marred by the extended smoke box so popular in the 1880's. (*Rogers Catalog*, p. 112)

55 The New York, Susquehanna and Western purchased this Mogul from Rogers in 1884 for freight service. (*Rogers Catalog*, p. 118)

56 The *106* conveys a feeling of ornamentation of an earlier generation of locomotive design. Built for the New York, New Haven and Hartford Railroad in 1882, she was a product of the New Haven shops. (*Scientific American,* May 16, 1885, p. 303)

57 The Schenectady Locomotive Works completed six Moguls for the Michigan Central in 1886. The *269* was the first in this group. It was retired in 1919. (*Railroad Gazette*, June 10, 1887)

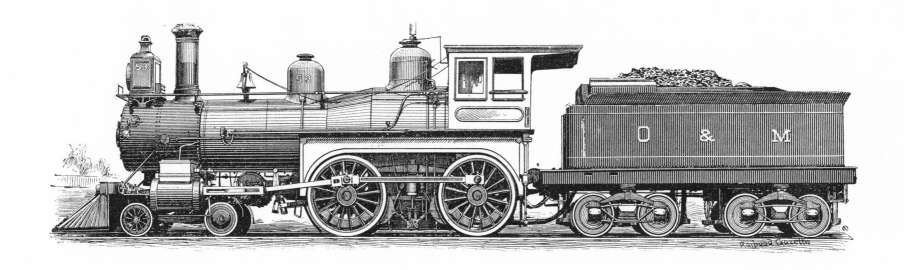

58 The reconstruction of locomotives has been mentioned elsewhere in these notes. It was a common practice that ranged from heavy repairs to extensive alterations in form. The locomotive pictured here was rebuilt by the Ohio and Mississippi Railroad at their shops in Vincennes, Indiana in 1888. Unfortunately the style and make of the original was not given in the article that accompanied the engraving. (*Railroad Gazette*, Oct. 19, 1888, p. 681)

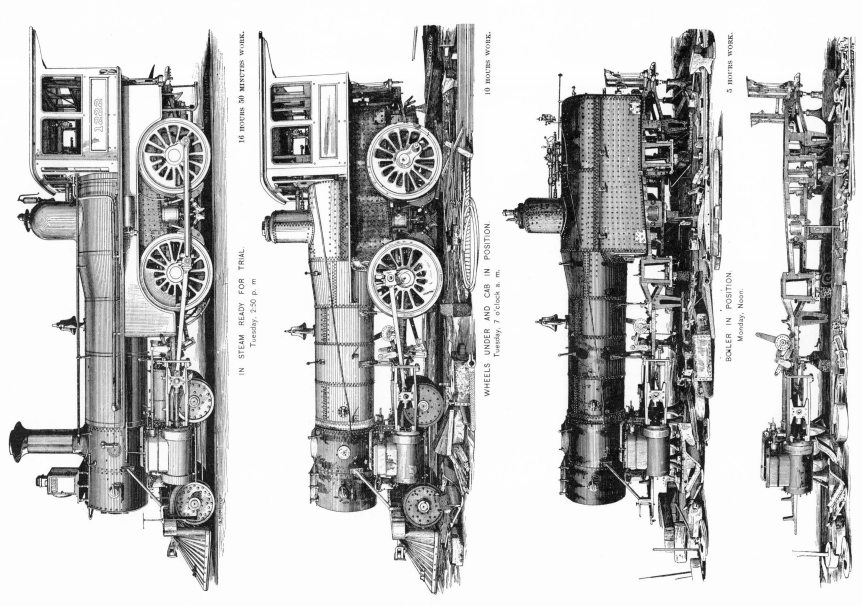

IN STEAM READY FOR TRIAL.
Tuesday, 2:50 p. m

16 HOURS 50 MINUTES WORK.

WHEELS UNDER AND CAB IN POSITION.
Tuesday, 7 o'clock a. m.

10 HOURS WORK.

BOILER IN POSITION.
Monday, Noon.

5 HOURS WORK.

COMMENCEMENT.
Monday, 7 o'clock a. m.

59 This engraving was intended to illustrate the quick assembly of a locomotive at the Altoona shops. To the modern viewer it presents an easily-understood explanation of railway engine construction. The Pennsylvania's 1212, built in 1888, was a class D7a passenger locomotive, a standard design introduced in 1882. (*Railroad Gazette*, Aug. 31, 1888)

60 The Lake Shore and Michigan Southern's *No. 220* was a high-speed passenger locomotive of the ordinary eight-wheel pattern. This comparatively light style of locomotive was used for express service on level lines until about 1900. The *220* was built by the Brooks Locomotive Works, Dunkirk, New York, in 1888 and was retired in 1918. (*Railroad Gazette*, Nov. 16, 1888)

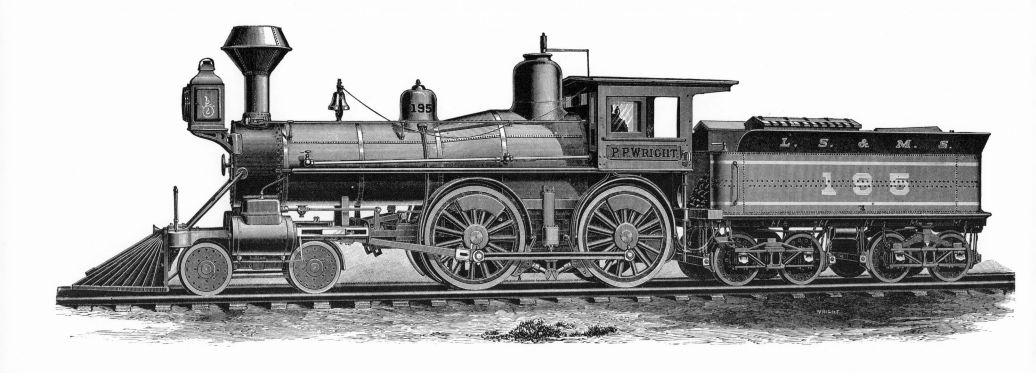

61 Another Lake Shore flyer was the *195* built in 1886 by Schenectady. It made a fast run with a seven-car train between Buffalo and Chicago in fourteen hours and five minutes (including stops). This machine and the *220* previously described were designed by George W. Stevens (1847–190?), the road's master mechanic from 1883 to 1899. (*Railroad Gazette*, March 11, 1887, opp. p. 162)

62 The Chicago, Milwaukee and St. Paul Railroad wanted heavier power than standard eight wheelers for fast passenger trains. Ten-wheel engines were commonly used to answer this need, but the *796* was fitted with a pair of trailing wheels that appear to be an afterthought. Some locomotive historians might argue that this machine was an early example of a Pacific type. The *796* was manufactured by Schenectady in 1889. (*Railroad Gazette*, Oct. 25, 1889, p. 693)

63 The ten thousandth locomotive built at the Baldwin Locomotive Works was this heavy Consolidation freight locomotive. The *10,000* was completed in June 1889 for the Northern Pacific Railway, and stayed in service until 1934. Baldwin's five thousandth machine had been built only nine years earlier. See Fig. 92. (*Scientific American Supplement*, Dec. 7, 1889, p. 11611)

64 This engraving and the following ones through Fig. 90 represent locomotives shown at the 1893 Columbian Exposition. The first of this group is the Baltimore and Ohio Railroad's *859*, an eight-wheel passenger locomotive outfitted with Vauclain compound cylinders.

Originally built by Baldwin, the *859* was rebuilt with conventional cylinders in 1905 and was retired in 1926. It was part of the B & O historical collection until about 1942 when it was donated to the scrap drive. (*Dredge*, Plate XXII, Fig. 2)

65 The biggest engine at the World's Fair was Baldwin's 97-ton Decapod. The New York, Lake Erie and Western was a short-lived corporate title of the Erie Railway resulting from one of its several reorganizations. (*Dredge*, Plate XXIII, Fig. 1)

66 Another Vauclain compound shown by Baldwin was this high-wheel Columbia type. Eleven similar machines were built for the Philadelphia and Reading between 1892 and 1893. The wheel arrangement was not successful and all engines of this class were remodeled along conventional lines within a few years. (*Dredge*, Plate XXIV, Fig. 1)

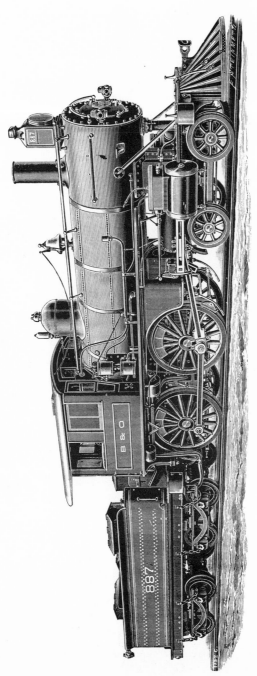

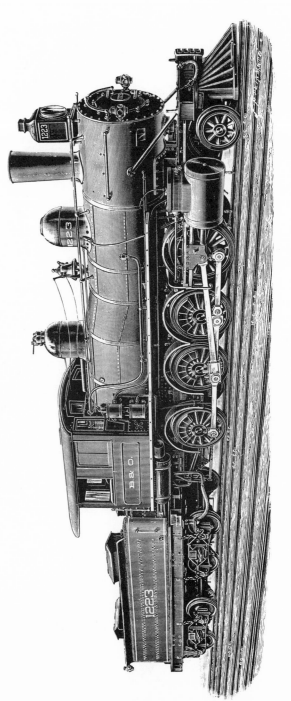

67 More conventional locomotives in the Baldwin exhibit were these three Baltimore and Ohio engines. The *858* and *887* were standard eight-wheel passenger locomotives of the day. The *1223* was a stock Consolidation freight engine. (*Dredge*, Plate XXVI, Figs. 1–3)

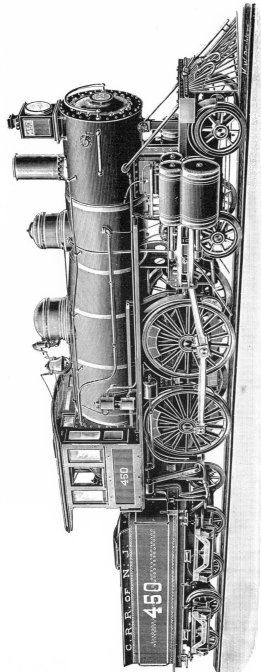

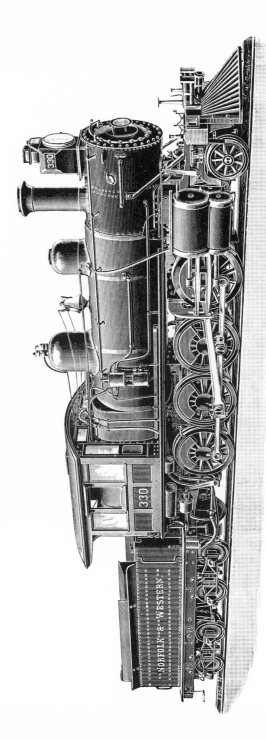

68 Three more Baldwin exhibits are shown in this plate. The B & O's *1342* was an uncommonly handsome Ten Wheeler that enjoyed a long service history. The Central of New Jersey's *450* went through two major rebuildings before its retirement in June 1929. The Norfolk and Western, which built much of its own power in later years, eventually put the *330* to work in the coal fields of Virginia. (*Dredge,* Plate XXVII, Figs. 1–3)

69 The Baltimore and Ohio South Western, the B & O's western line, between Cincinnati and St. Louis, was formerly the Ohio and Mississippi Railroad. The *123* was part of the Baldwin exhibit. (*Dredge*, Plate XXVIII, Fig. 1)

70 The final engraving from the Baldwin exhibit is this sturdy Mogul freight locomotive. It was built specifically for the exhibit and was sold to Lima Northern Railroad as their *No. 61* after the fair closed. In all, Baldwin showed sixteen locomotives. (*Dredge*, Plate XXIX, Fig. 1)

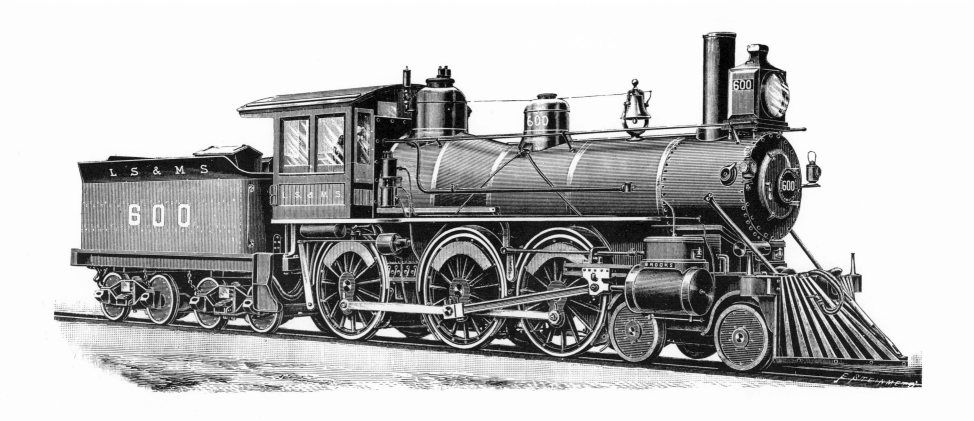

71 The Brooks Locomotive Works of Dunkirk, New York, was the second largest exhibitor of railway engines at the Columbian fair. It showed nine machines. Among these was a standard ten-wheel passenger engine for the Lake Shore and Michigan Southern Railway. (*Dredge*, Plate XXXII, Fig. 1)

72 Brooks built the *210* for the Cincinnati, Hamilton and Dayton Railroad, a B & O subsidiary line running along the Ohio and Indiana border between Cincinnati and Toledo. The *210* was notable for its electric headlight. (*Dredge*, Plate XXXII, Fig. 3)

73 The Great Northern was a valued customer of Brooks as shown by the several locomotives represented in these pages. The *No. 410* was a freight locomotive of the Mastodon type, a relatively little-used style of locomotive in this country. (*Dredge*, Plate XXXIII, Fig. 1)

74 In contrast, the Great Northern's *515* was of the immensely popular Consolidation type. The engine was a four-cylinder compound after the plan of Brooks's superintendent, John Player. (*Dredge,* Plate XXXIII, Fig. 3)

75 The *599* was one of five heavy eight wheelers produced for the Lake Shore by Brooks. Its sisters hauled the Exposition Flyer, a 19-hour New York to Chicago train, while the *599* reposed at the World's Fair. (*Dredge*, Plate XXXIV, Fig. 1)

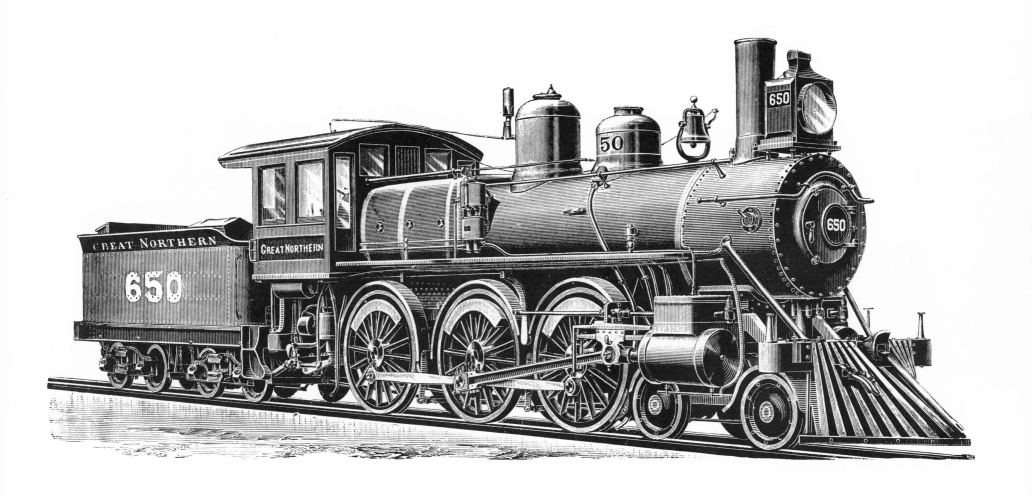

76 The Great Northern's *650* was a conventional ten-wheel passenger locomotive of its day. It formed part of Brooks's exhibit. (*Dredge*, Plate XXXIX, Fig. 1)

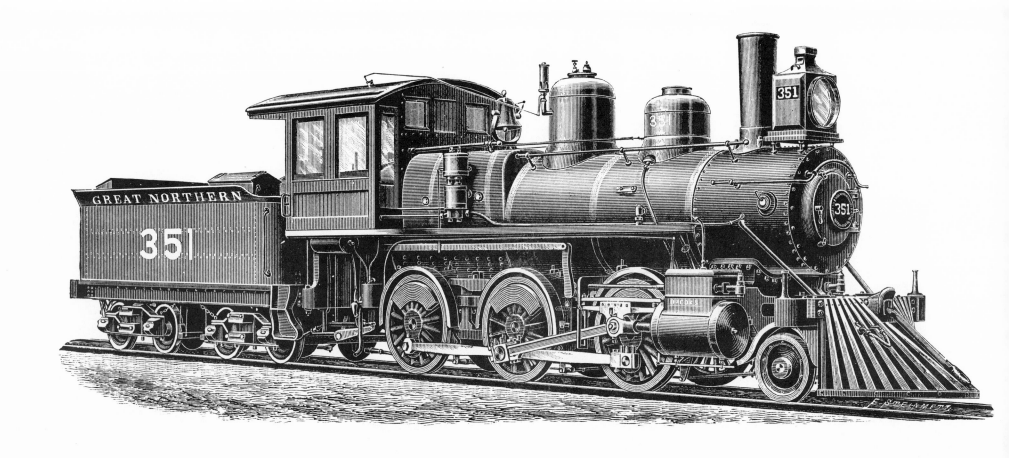

77 The *351* was yet another Brooks entry at the Columbian Exposition. It was a middle-weight freight locomotive of the Mogul type, built for the Great Northern. By this time, this wheel arrangement had largely fallen from favor in America for main line service although it continued to be produced for many years. (*Dredge*, Plate XXXIX, Fig. 3)

78   The Canadian Pacific was represented at the Columbian by the *626*. The metal cab was a notable feature for the time. It had been built in the Montreal shops of that company and appears to follow a general design developed in 1889 by Francis R. F. Brown, a Scotsman who was mechanical superintendent on the C. P. between about 1883 and 1890. Other sources give the number of the engine exhibited as *456* and *625*. (*Dredge*, p. 166, Fig. 47)

79 A leading attraction at the Exposition was the New York Central and Hudson River Railroad's famed *999*. This machine had created a sensation just a few months before by reaching a speed of 112.5 m.p.h. between Batavia and Buffalo, New York, while pulling the Empire State Express. During its long years of service the *999* underwent many rebuildings. It survives today in a much altered form at the Chicago Museum of Science and Industry. (*Dredge*, Plate LI, Fig. 1)

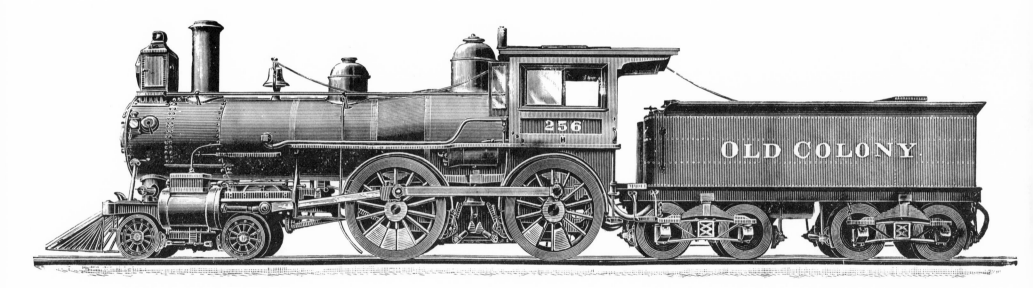

80 The Old Colony Railroad built the *256* at its own shops in Boston in 1893. After its brief rest at the Columbian Exposition, the *256* returned to service and continued its labors until 1925. (*Dredge,* p.241, Fig. 61)

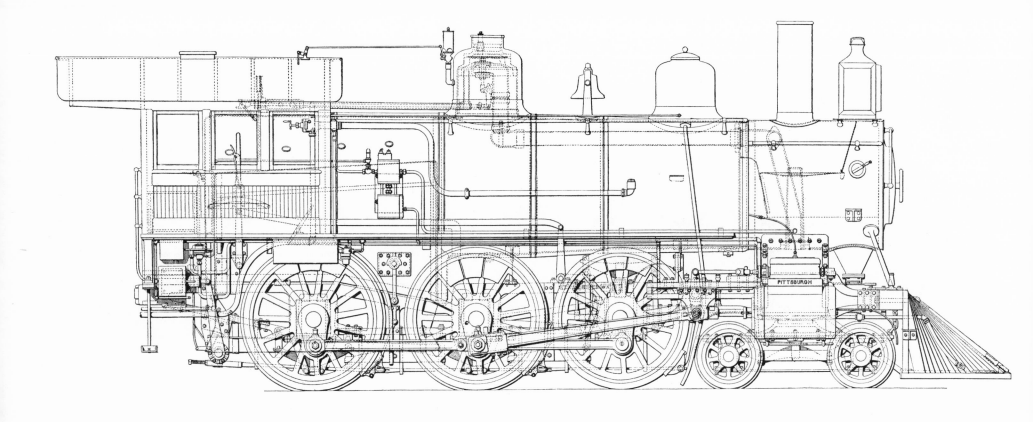

81 The Pittsburgh Locomotive Works exhibited a ten-wheel passenger engine it had built for the Terre Haute and Indianapolis Railroad.

The Vandalia was one of the Pennsylvania Railroad's Lines West. (*Dredge*, Plate LX, Fig. 1)

82 The Chicago, Milwaukee and St. Paul Railway acquired a second group of modified ten wheelers from the Rhode Island Locomotive Works (Providence) in 1893. The first of their spurious Pacific types was shown in Figure 62. The *830* and her sisters were not satisfactory and were returned to their maker. In about 1900 they were sold to the Plant System which ordered two of them rebuilt as simple engines. All had been originally constructed as Batchellor cross compounds. In later years the three were remodelled as Ten Wheelers. They were cut up in May 1934. (*Dredge*, Plate LXI, Fig. 1)

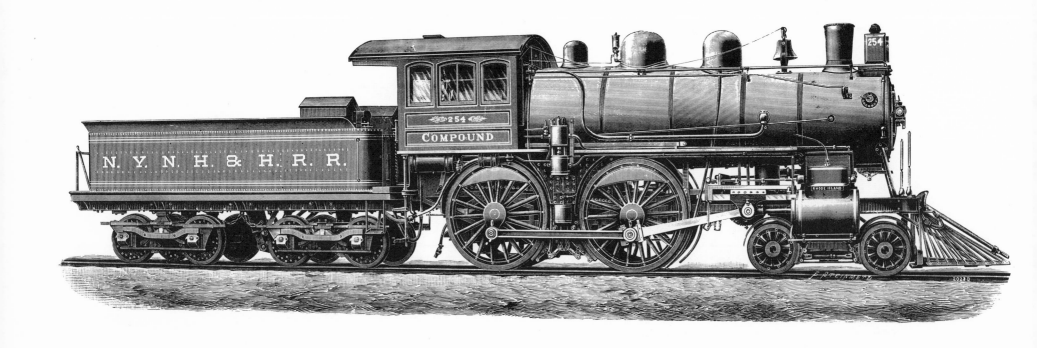

83 The *254* was one of sixteen class C-15a locomotives built in 1893 for the New York, New Haven and Hartford Railroad by the Rhode Island Locomotive Works. The *254* and its sisters were cross compounds. The general design was by John Henney, Jr., locomotive superintendent for the New Haven. (*Dredge*, Plate LXII, Fig. 1)

84 Rhode Island's thinking for a compound freight locomotive was represented by the Minneapolis, St. Paul and Sault Ste. Marie's *No.* *400.* It too employed the Batchellor cross compound system. (*Dredge,* Plate LXIII, Fig. 1)

85 Richmond was the only southern city to have a major locomotive plant. The works, started in 1865 as a farm machinery business, entered locomotive production several years later. It continued its operations until 1927. At the Columbian fair they were represented by a single exhibit, this Chesapeake and Ohio Consolidation freight engine, the *350*. (*Dredge*, Plate LXV, Fig. 1)

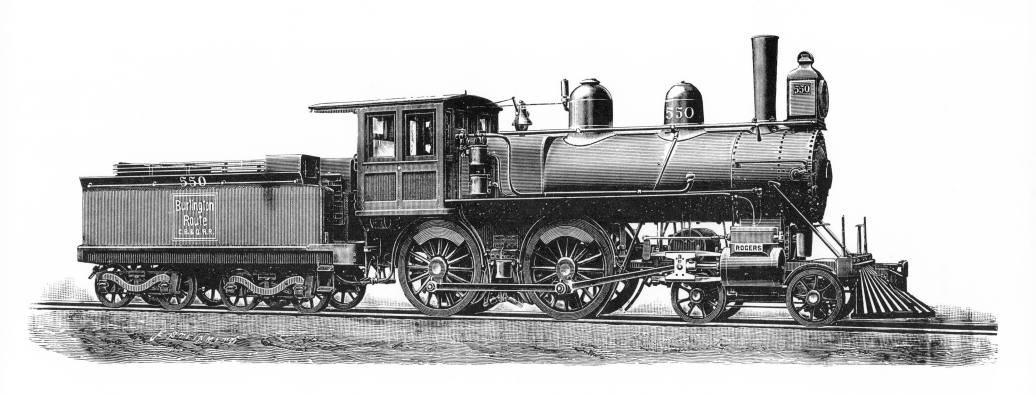

86 In the early 1890's the Chicago, Burlington and Quincy Railroad decided to stay with the dependable eight wheeler for its passenger trains. Typical of these machines was the *550* built by Rogers to the road's standard class M design. Rogers exhibited this engine at the Columbian Exposition. (*Dredge*, p. 272, Fig. 73)

87 This high-wheeled passenger engine was another Rogers product shown at the Columbian. It was built for a conglomerate of southern railroads assembled in the 1880's and 1890's by Henry B. Plant, a Connecticut Yankee. (*Dredge*, p. 285, Fig. 74)

88 The Chicago and North Western's *400*, like the Plant System's *100* just shown, was a ten-wheel passenger locomotive. The engine lost its name *Columbus* when entering regular service at the end of the fair. The *400* was built by the Schenectady Locomotive Works. It was retired in 1926. (*Dredge*, Plate LXIX, Fig. 1)

89 The Duluth and Iron Range's twelve-wheel freight locomotive *No. 60* was another of the four Schenectady exhibit engines. Weighing 84.5 tons, it was the second heaviest locomotive shown at the Columbian. (*Dredge*, Plate LXX, Fig. 1)

90 The Mohawk and Malone Railroad, a subsidiary of the New York Central and Hudson River Railroad, purchased this Consolidation freight locomotive in 1893. It was shown by the Schenectady Locomotive Works at the Chicago World's Fair to advertise a cross compound system developed by Albert J. Pitkin, later president of the American Locomotive Company. (*Dredge*, Plate LXXI, Fig. 1)

91 This unusual friction drive locomotive was built to the patented design of Eugene Fontaine in 1881 by the Grant Locomotive Works for the Canada Southern Railroad. After an unsuccessful career as a demonstrator the engine was rebuilt along conventional lines for the Wheeling and Lake Erie Railroad. (*Recent Locomotives*, Fig. 48)

92 More conventional than Fontaine's locomotive, the Reading's *507* was considered peculiar because of its single pair of driving wheels. The engine was returned to Baldwin soon after completion in 1880 by the financially exhausted Reading. The builder resold it to the Eames Vacuum Brake Company to demonstrate that firm's system in Great Britain. The engine, renamed *Lovett Eames* in honor of the inventor's father, was scrapped in 1884 or 1885. (*Recent Locomotives*, Fig. 43)

93 The Central Pacific built the *236* at its shops in 1882 for commuter service out of Oakland. The engine was classified as a tank engine because the water was carried in rectangular tanks running astride the boiler, above the wheels. The fuel was carried in the hopper behind the cab and thus no tender was required. A sister of the *236* is presently exhibited in a park in Oakland, California. (*Recent Locomotives,* Fig. 81)

94 The Atchison, Topeka and Santa Fe's *Uncle Dick* was another style of tenderless engine known as a saddle tank because of the U-shaped water tank mounted on its boiler. Unusually large for a tank engine, it was used to push trains over a temporary switchback railroad in the Raton Mountains. Once the low level main line was completed, the *Uncle Dick* was assigned less strenuous duties. Delivered in 1878, it was the 4500th locomotive completed at the Baldwin Works. It was retired in 1921. (*Recent Locomotives*, Fig. 79)

95 The *Ariel* was the first two-foot gauge locomotive built in this country. It was completed in 1877 by the Hinkley Locomotive Works, Boston, for the Billerica and Bedford Railroad. The Massachusetts line soon failed, however, and the *Ariel* ended its days in Maine. It was renamed *Bo-peep* in its later years. (*Recent Locomotives,* Fig. 84)

96 Locomotives like the *Ariel* and New York Elevated *39* shown were called Forney type locomotives after the 1866 patent of M. N. Forney, a renowned locomotive expert of the time. Forney types were well adapted to light passenger service. The New York elevated lines used hundreds of these little machines before adopting electricity in the early years of this century. The *No. 39* was built by Baldwin in 1878. (*Recent Locomotives*, Fig. 92)

97 A heavier Forney type for main-line suburban service is illustrated by the New York and Harlem Railroad's *26*. Built in 1876 by the Schenectady Locomotive Works, it was rebuilt as a four-wheel switcher in 1899. (*Recent Locomotives*, Fig. 95)

98 The *Breckenridge*, though similar in appearance to Forney's plan, is actually another variety of tank engine known as a Mason double truck locomotive. It was an articulated locomotive developed by William Mason of Taunton, Massachusetts, from the British Fairlie design. The *Breckenridge* was built in 1879 for the Denver, South Park and Pacific Railroad. In later years it ran on the Utah & Northern. (*Recent Locomotives*, Fig. 104)

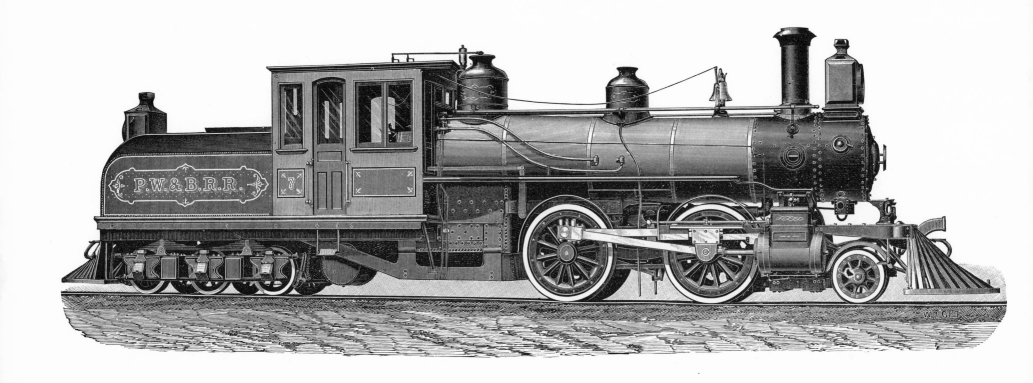

99 A later version of Mason double truck locomotive is shown by the *Pokanoket* of the Providence, Warren and Bristol Railroad. It was built in 1885 and scrapped in 1906. In all, Mason built about 150 double truck locomotives. (*Recent Locomotives,* Fig. 355)

100 The P. W. & B. favored unusual names as well as unusual locomotive design. The *Annawomscutt* was an 1887 product of the Taunton Locomotive Manufacturing Company. Its peculiar wheel arrangement was apparently not successful for it was rebuilt as a four-wheel engine in 1891. (*Catechism of the Locomotive*, 1890 Ed., Fig. 106)

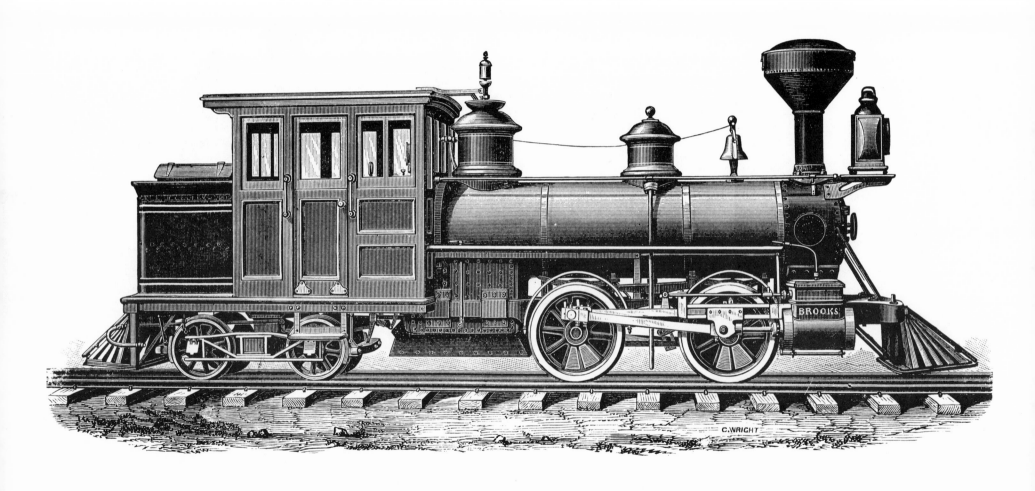

101 Brooks offered this eight-wheel, narrow-gauge Forney type as a standard design in the mid 1880's. A specific purchaser cannot be named. (*Recent Locomotives*, Fig. 90)

102 The Rhode Island Locomotive Works built five 37-ton Forney engines for the Evansville, Washington and Worthington Railroad in March of 1880. Before delivery could be made, the railroad failed. It was reorganized as the Indianapolis and Evansville Railroad. This line was eventually abosrbed by the Chicago and Eastern Illinois. (*Recent Locomotives*, Fig. 93)

103 The Porter locomotive works of Pittsburgh specialized in light locomotives for industrial and logging railroads. Typical of its products was the little engine shown here. It was built in 1884 probably for the Saginaw Bay and North Western Railroad, a line later leased by the Michigan Central. (*Recent Locomotives*, Fig. 366)

104 Grant built five light passenger locomotives of this type for Central Railroad of New Jersey in 1872. They were intended for suburban trains but the same machines were also called gravel engines, indicating their use for construction or maintenance of way service. The small truck wheels at either end facilitated easy travel in both directions. (*Weissenborn*, Plate XXXXIV)

105 The Illinois Central operated a large suburban service south from Chicago. Before electric cars were introduced dozens of steam tank engines hauled these trains. The *213* was built by Rogers in 1880. A sister engine exhibited for many years in the Chicago Museum of Science and Industry is still in existence. (*Rogers Catalog* p. 164)

106 The smallest American locomotive illustrated in these pages is this 20-inch gauge four-wheel tank engine built in 1880 by Porter for the Longfellow Mining Company of Arizona. The tiny machine weighted only 4½ tons; its driving wheels were 22 inches in diameter. (*Recent Locomotives*, Fig. 106)

107 Slightly larger was this steel mill engine built by Pittsburgh in 1893. It outweighed the *Coronada* by 2 tons. It was shown at the Columbian Exposition but its later history is not known. (*Dredge*, p. 253, Fig. 64)

108 Even the largest locomotive manufacturers, Baldwin included, produced small, cheap engines for industrial service. This little saddle tanker was part of Baldwin's display at the Columbian Exposition. At the close of the fair it was sold to the New Mexico Railway and Coal Company. (*Dredge*, Plate XXXI, Fig. 1)

109 Since the 1870's, low silhouette tank engines were used in mines. They were, of course, only practical for large or well-ventilated mines. They burned coke or hard coal to reduce smoke. For better clearance, they were built low to the ground. The cylinders were placed inside the frame, under the boiler, to reduce the engine's width. This machine was produced in about 1885 by the Dickson Manufacturing Company of Scranton, Pennsylvania. (*Recent Locomotives*, Fig. 374)

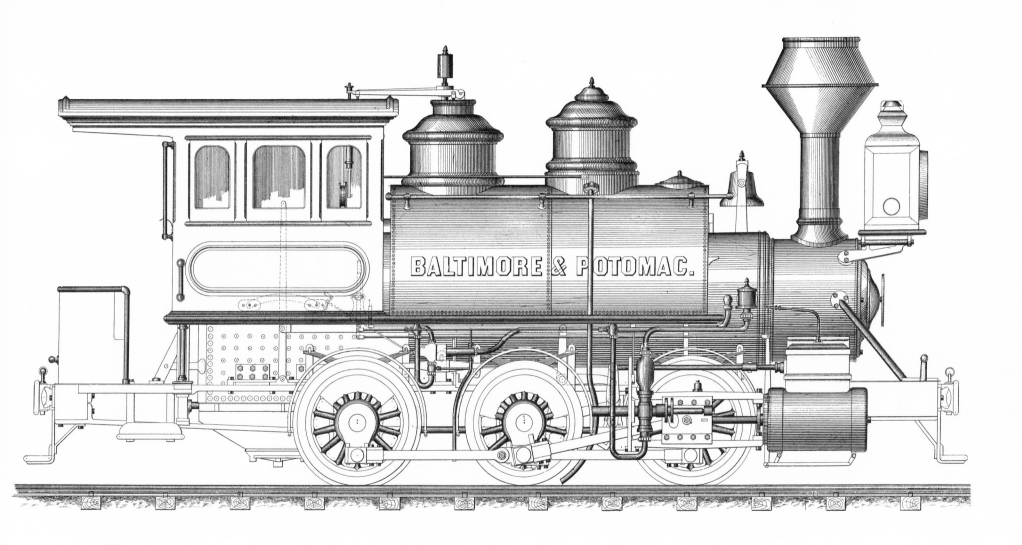

110 The Baltimore and Potomac's *22* was completed in March 1873 by Baldwin. It was classified as a saddle tank engine because of the U-shaped tank mounted astride the boiler. This arrangement was used by small industrial and switching locomotives to avoid the necessity of a separate tender. Such machines made short runs and were usually close to supplies of water and fuel. The B & P was built in the early 1870's by the Pennsylvania Railroad as an extension to Washington, D. C. and the South. (*Weissenborn*, Plate LXVIII)

111 After the opening of the Mt. Washington Cog Railway in New Hampshire, rack railways were built in all parts of the world. One such line was the Prince of Grand Pará Railroad in Brazil. The locomotive shown here was built by Baldwin in 1886. It used the Riggenbach (Swiss) system of cog gearing to overcome the 15-percent grades. (*Recent Locomotives,* Fig. 373)

112 Adams and Price of Nashville produced this chain drive engine for a saw mill in Alabama in 1884. It was intended for slow speed operations on "pole roads," a cheap form of railway constructed from tree trunks. Note the cup shaped wheels necessary to traverse such lines. Similar engines were produced in Richmond, Virginia. The design was after a patent of W. E. Cole. (*Recent Locomotives*, Fig. 369)

113 Another and more widely used style of logging locomotive was the Shay geared engine produced from 1880 to 1945 by the Lima Locomotive Works, Lima, Ohio. The *450* shown here was exhibited at the Columbian Exposition. It was sold to the Hardwick and Woodbury Railroad after the fair. The *450* spent its last years on an Alabama lumber road. (*Dredge*, Plate LXXV, Fig. 1)

114 The following five illustrations depict standard American switching engines. These machines were typically fitted with small driving wheels and no leading or trailing wheels. Rogers built this engine in 1879 for the Haydenville Branch Railroad. (*Rogers Catalog*, p. 138)

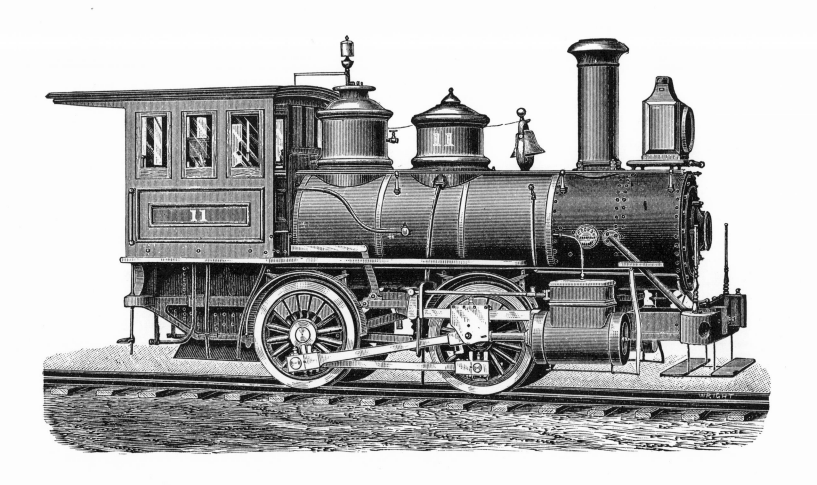

115 Another four-wheel yard goat was this Cooke engine of about 1885. Cooke was another locomotive manufacturer located in Paterson, New Jersey. The purchaser of the *No. 11* cannot be determined. (*Catechism of the Locomotive*, p. 128)

116 Rogers produced the *21* for the Georgia Railroad in 1877. Six-wheel switchers were beginning to displace four-wheel engines for heavier yard shifting assignments. Some railroads, incidentally, called switchers "drill" engines. Note also the slope-back tender, a favored form of water tank for switchers because it afforded greater visibility when running backwards. (*Rogers Catalog*, p. 144)

117 A heavier six-wheel switcher was produced in 1893 for the Chicago and North Western Railway by the Schenectady Locomotive Works. The *140* was part of Schenectady's exhibit at the Columbian World's Fair. It continued in service until 1925. (*Dredge*, Plate LXXIV, Fig. 1)

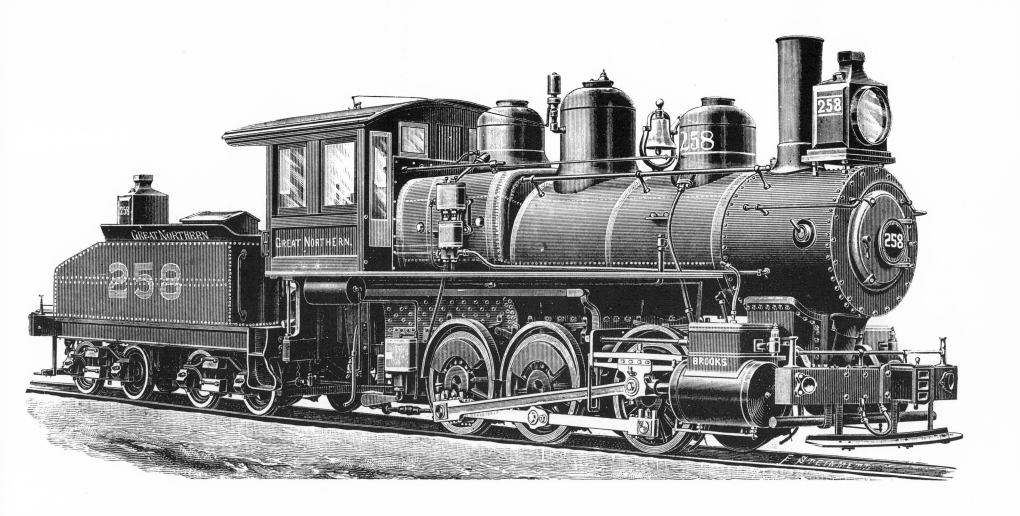

118 Another humble shifter that made it to the World's Fair was the Great Northern's *258*. It was part of the Brooks exhibit. Eight- and even ten-wheel switchers were introduced after about 1905 for heavier yard work. But six-wheelers like the *258* remained the most popular form of switching engine on American railroads until the advent of diesel-electrics in the 1930's. (*Dredge*, Plate XXXIX, Fig. 2)

119 Before the perfection of electric street traction in the 1880's, American city railways tried many exotic forms of power in an effort to displace horse-propelled cars. In the 1870's the Crescent City Railway of New Orleans tried some steam storage motors built in Paterson, New Jersey, by Theodore Scheffler in 1876. These locomotives were fireless and obtained a "charge" of steam from a stationary boiler house. In later years a limited number of fireless locomotives were used for industrial railways. A few may be seen in service today around electric generating plants. (*Recent Locomotives,* Fig. 110)

120 This delightful inspection locomotive of 1871 was surely a pet of the roundhouse crew. Most large railroads had one or more such machines for official inspection tours. Some railroads had steam cars of this same general type in service as late as the 1930's. The *Star* was cut up in 1899. William Woodcock (d. 1886) designed the *Star* at the Elizabethport shops soon after being named Master Mechanic of the Central Railroad of New Jersey. (*Weissenborn*, Plate XXXXVIII)

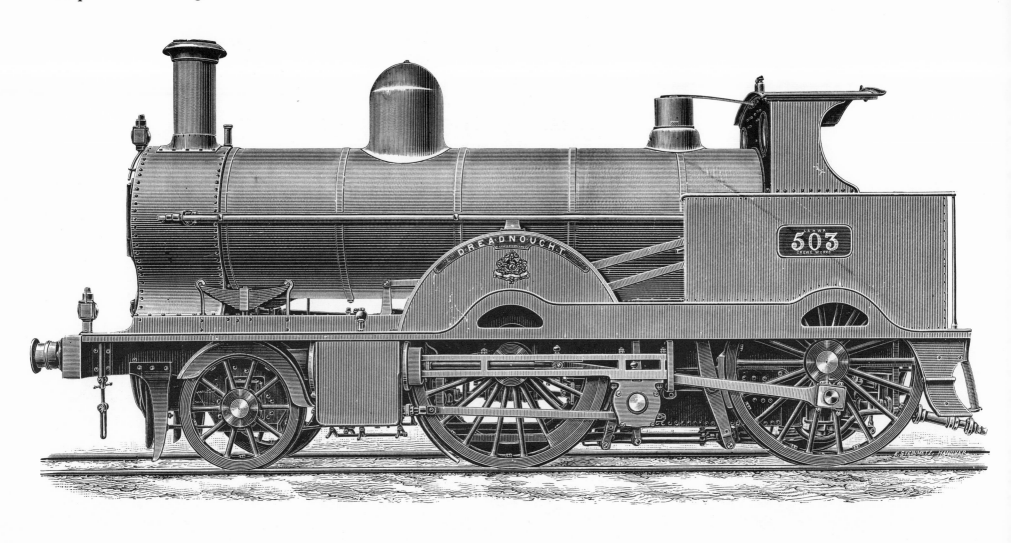

121 Francis W. Webb (1835–1904), long-time motive power superin-tendent of the London and North Western Railway, built the *503* in 1884 in Crewe, England. It was an early example of his three-cylinder compound introduced just two years before. (*Dredge*, Plate XLIII)

122 The *1301* was another Webb compound built at the Crewe Shops of the London and North Western. Completed in 1889, it was exhibited at the Columbian Exposition. A similar machine was made in England for tests on the Pennsylvania Railroad in the same year. (*Dredge*, Plate XLVII)

123 This engraving was captioned "Dignity and Impudence" by a Victorian editor. The *Nipper* was a toy size, 18-inch-gauge shop switcher at the London and North Western's Crewe Shops. Its big brother, a veteran dating back to 1847, is shown after an 1858 remodeling. The *Cornwall* has been preserved by the British Transport Commission. (*Recent Locomotives*, Fig. 179)

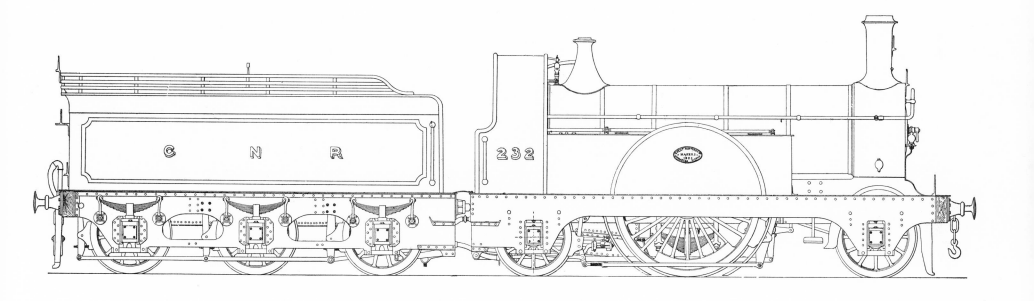

124 The Great Northern Railway's *232* was another British express locomotive with a single pair of driving wheels. It was a favorite form of passenger engine in England and prevailed until train weights grew beyond its capacity. The *232* was built by the Great Northern Shops at Doncaster in 1885. (*Recent Locomotives*, Fig. 439)

125 The *128* was built in about 1881 by Neilson and Company, Glasgow, for the Caledonian Railway. This is an American-type locomotive modeled on our standard eight-wheel arrangement. The British were at first reluctant to accept the leading truck. After 1870 they were more widely used for passenger locomotives in England. (*Recent Locomotives,* Fig. 127)

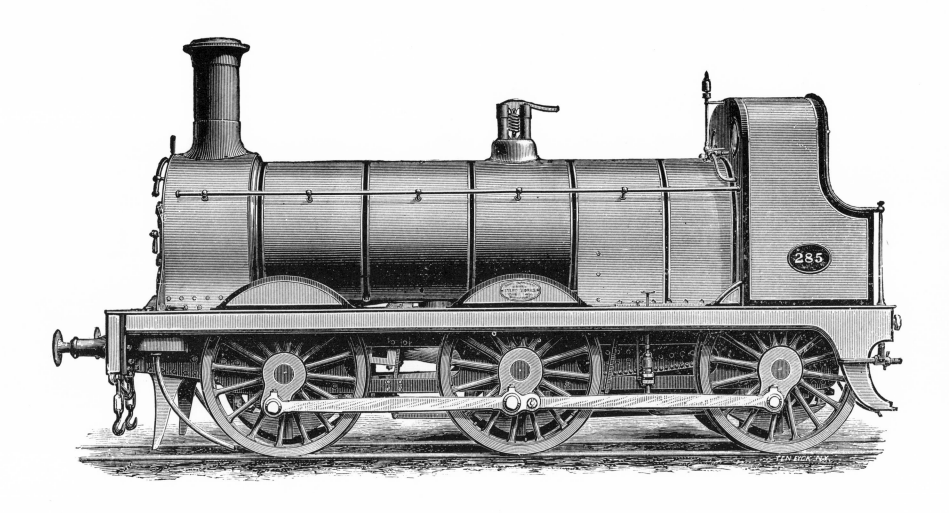

126 The standard English freight locomotive for most of the nineteenth century was the "six-wheel goods engine." A typical example is the Southeastern Railway's *285*. It was built in about 1882 by Sharp, Stewart & Company, Manchester. James Stirling, the designer of the *285*, was the brother of the celebrated Patrick Stirling (1820–1895), a locomotive expert of international reputation. (*Recent Locomotives*, Fig. 134)

127 Six-wheel engines were also used for local passenger service in England. The London, Brighton and South Coast Railway acquired engines of this design in 1872. They were so satisfactory that fifty were in service within ten years. They became known as "Terriers" because of their snappy performance. William Stroudley (1833–1889), superintendent of the Brighton line, prepared the design. (*Recent Locomotives*, Fig. 138)

128 This eight-wheel tank engine was another popular suburban locomotive in Britain. The Northeastern Railway built or acquired a large number built to the design of Edward Fletcher between 1874 and 1883. The example shown here was built by Neilson & Company. We would classify this style of locomotive a Forney type. (*Recent Locomotives*, Fig. 166)

129 The *No. 35* of the Great Southern and Western Railway of Ireland was built in 1879 at the company's shops. It was a double truck engine much like that shown in the preceding figure but it was articulated after the general designs of R.F. Fairlie. *See Figs. 30 and 98 for other examples of Fairlies. (Recent Locomotives, Fig. 168)*

130 This odd-looking ten-wheel tank engine was made in 1886 by Beyer, Peacock & Company, Manchester, England, for the Mersey River Tunnel Railway. The tunnel line offered a connection between Liverpool and Birkenhead. At 76 tons, this was a very large locomotive for its time. (*Recent Locomotives*, Fig. 466)

131 The *James Toleman* was a freakish experiment that incorporated many novel but not necessarily practical ideas. Its four-cylinder drive and elliptical boiler won it few admirers. It was built in 1892 by Hawthorne, Leslie & Company (Newcastle, England) to the order of its designer, F. C. Winby. It was shown at the Columbian Exposition. After the fair closed, it was tested on the Milwaukee Road but was soon placed in storage. In about 1900 the *Toleman* was given to Purdue University for its proposed but never opened railway museum. Its final disposition is not recorded. (*Dredge*, Plate LXXX)

132 Four French locomotives were shown at the Columbian Exposition. One of them was the Western Railway of France's six-wheel tank locomotive, the *3535*. It was made by the Compagnie de Fives-Lille in about 1885 for suburban service. (*Dredge*, p. 319, Fig. 103)

133 Locomotives of this wheel arrangement were extremely popular with continental railways for both freight and passenger service. The example shown here was built in about 1875 for the Württemberg State Railway by the Esslingen Machine Works, Esslingen, Germany. (*Recent Locomotives*, Fig. 482)

134 This simple four-wheel locomotive was built for the Swiss Northeastern Railroad by Esslingen in 1874. (*Recent Locomotives,* Fig. 483)

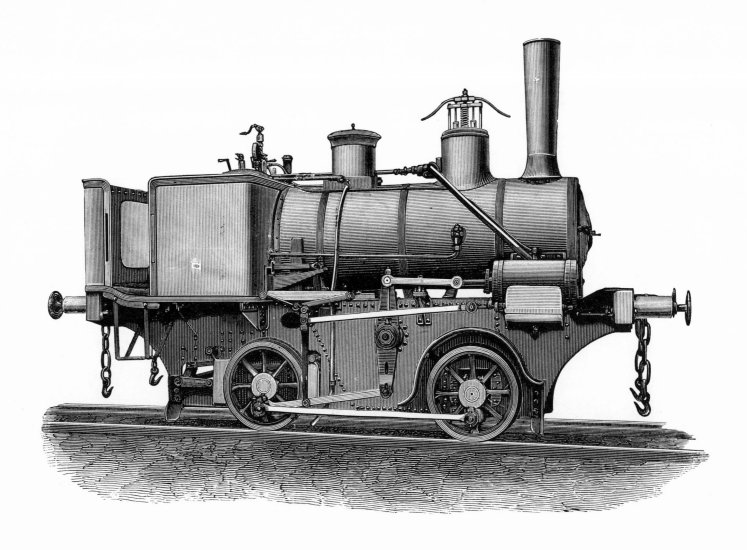

135 Many mechanics labored to perfect a compensating lever locomotive. One such effort was this 1878 machine designed by Charles Brown (1827-1905) of the Swiss Locomotive Works, Winterthur. Brown was an Englishman who spent much of his life in Switzerland. Locomotives of this arrangement ran more smoothly than ordinary direct connected engines, but the added machinery discouraged a general acceptance of the scheme. (*Recent Locomotives,* Fig. 176)

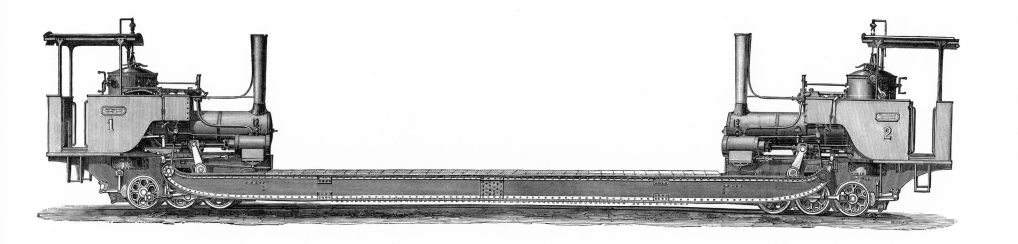

136 This remarkable double locomotive was also the product of Charles Brown and also featured a lever drive. It was built in 1878 at Brown's Winterthur factory for the narrow-gauge Villa Real and Villa Regoa tramway in Portugal. (*Recent Locomotives*, Fig. 175)

137 Although part of the British Empire, New Zealand bought a number of locomotives from American manufacturers. Our locomotives were more suitable to the requirements of most colonial railways. These lines copied our practice or in some cases purchased directly from U. S. manufacturers. To hold these markets British manufacturers were forced to emulate our designs. The *Washington* was one of eight built by Rogers in 1877–1878 for the New Zealand Railway. All were retired by 1928. (*Rogers Catalog*, p. 188)

138 Another New Zealand import was this Baldwin Prairie type of 1885. Baldwin exported its first locomotive in 1838. By the 1870's foreign orders were an important part of its business. Engines were sent to all parts of the world but the major trade was with South America. (*Recent Locomotives*, Fig. 243)

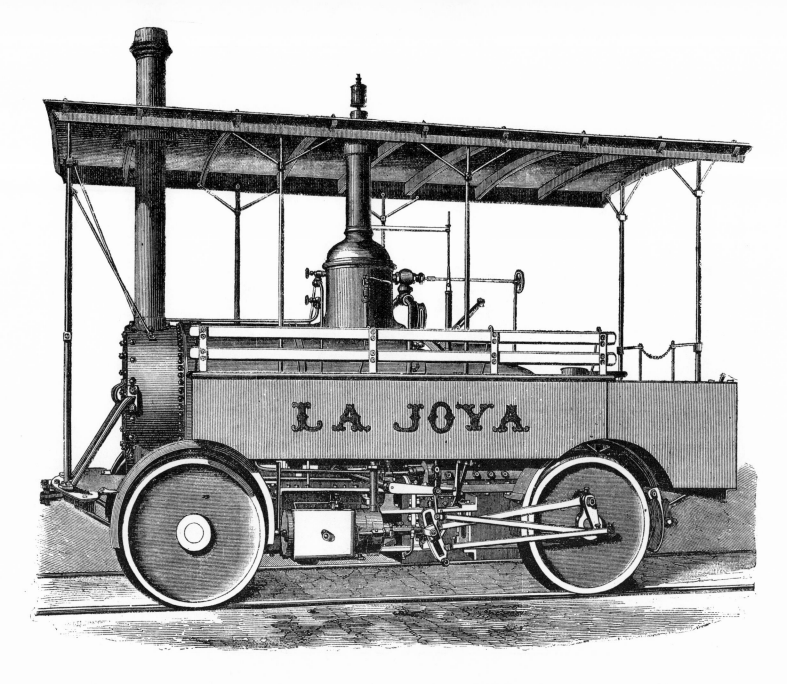

139 This steam inspection car might not properly qualify as a locomotive but we doubt if many readers will object to the inclusion of this charming cut. The *Joya* *(Jewel)* was built in July 1869 for Mejía and Arequipa Railway (Peru). Rogers had made a similar car for the Copiapo Railway (Chile) two years before. *(Scientific American,* Aug. 27, 1870, p. 130)

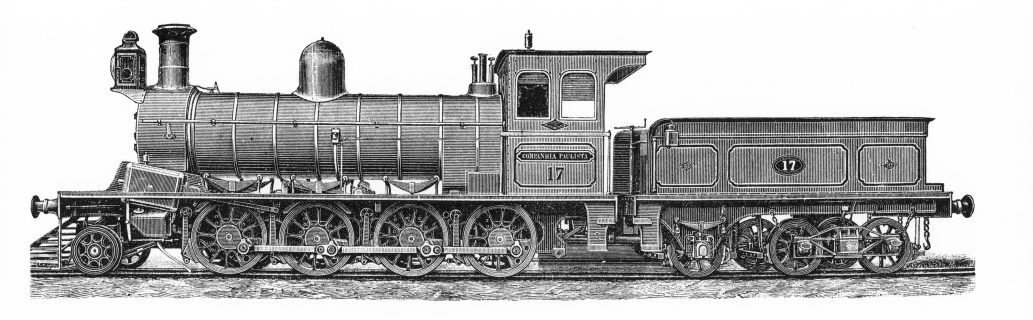

140 The Paulista Railroad of Brazil received this freight locomotive in 1884 from Dubs & Company, Glasgow. It corresponds to American design except for the placement of the cylinders inside of the frames. (*Recent Locomotives*, Fig. 473)

141 Baldwin built this heavy freight locomotive, a Decapod, for the Dom Pedro II Railway of Brazil in 1885. The gauge of this line was 5 feet 3 inches. After the 1889 revolution the line was called the Central Brazil. (*Recent Locomotives*, Fig. 353)

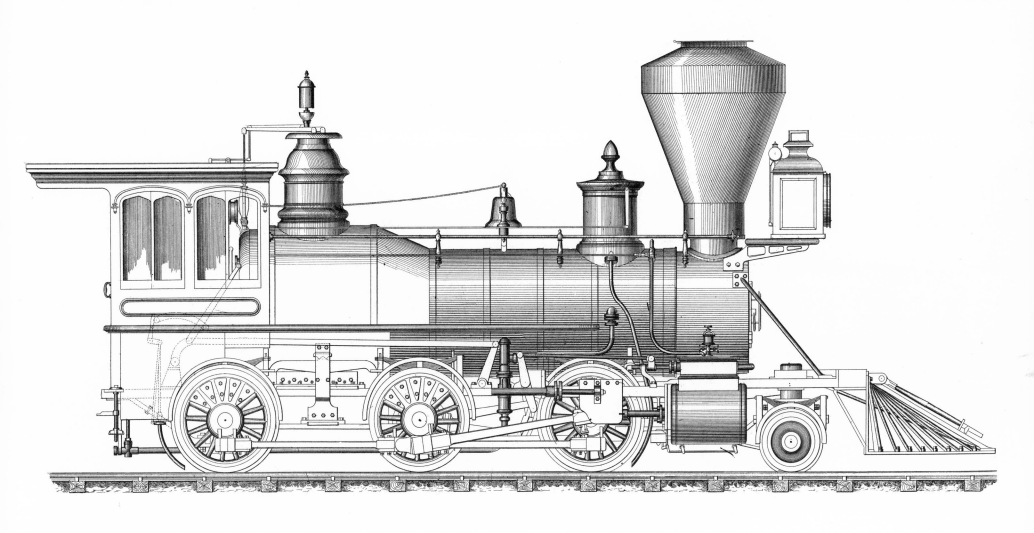

142 Danforth, Cooke & Company of Paterson, New Jersey, furnished six Mogul freight locomotives to the Mejía and Arequipa Railway (Peru) in August 1871. The first engine in this order was assigned the maker's construction number *750.* (*Weissenborn*, Plate XX)

143 This wood-burning ten wheeler was built in 1874 by Rogers for the Neuvitas and Puerto Príncipe Railway in Cuba. Rogers sent their first locomotive to Cuba in 1841 and became a major supplier of such machinery to that island in later years. (*Rogers Catalog*, p. 126)

144 In 1878 the Leopoldina Railway (Brazil) purchased this narrow-gauge freight locomotive from Rogers. The railway was named in honor of Emperor Leopold. (*Rogers Catalog*, p. 176)

145 The first locomotive for the Barão de Araucana Railway (Brazil) was completed in September 1878 by Rogers. This meter-gauge tank engine weighed 24½ tons. It could haul a 600-ton train on a level track. (*Rogers Catalog*, p. 186)

146 Rogers built this small four-wheel tank engine in 1875 for a South American firm. Location of the railway is not certain but it was probably an industrial or plantation line. (*Rogers Catalog,* p. 182)

147 The Matanzas Railroad (Cuba) acquired the *No. 32* from Rogers in 1878. The wheel arrangement is unusual, as is the six-wheel truck under the tank. The engine was designed as a double ender—notice the cowcatcher at both ends—and could operate safely in either direction. (*Rogers Catalog*, p. 192)